50 TWO-HAND TAPPING WORKOUTS
FOR ELECTRIC BASS

BY CHRIS MATHEOS

Online Audio www.melbay.com/99365MEB

AUDIO CONTENTS

CONTENTS

50 TWO-HAND TAPPING WORKOUTS FOR ELECTRIC BASS

Two-hand tapping on electric bass is very similar to playing piano. Your right and left hands both play notes. This is a fairly new concept on bass. New techniques and ideas are being created regularly. Tapping is being applied to all sorts of musical styles including: blues, alternative, jazz, funk, and even classical. Try applying the techniques in this book to your favorite styles of music. Expand on the exercises. Maybe you'll create a new sound or technique.

MEL BAY® QWIKGUIDE®

2 3 4 5 6 7 8 9 0

EXAMPLE 1:

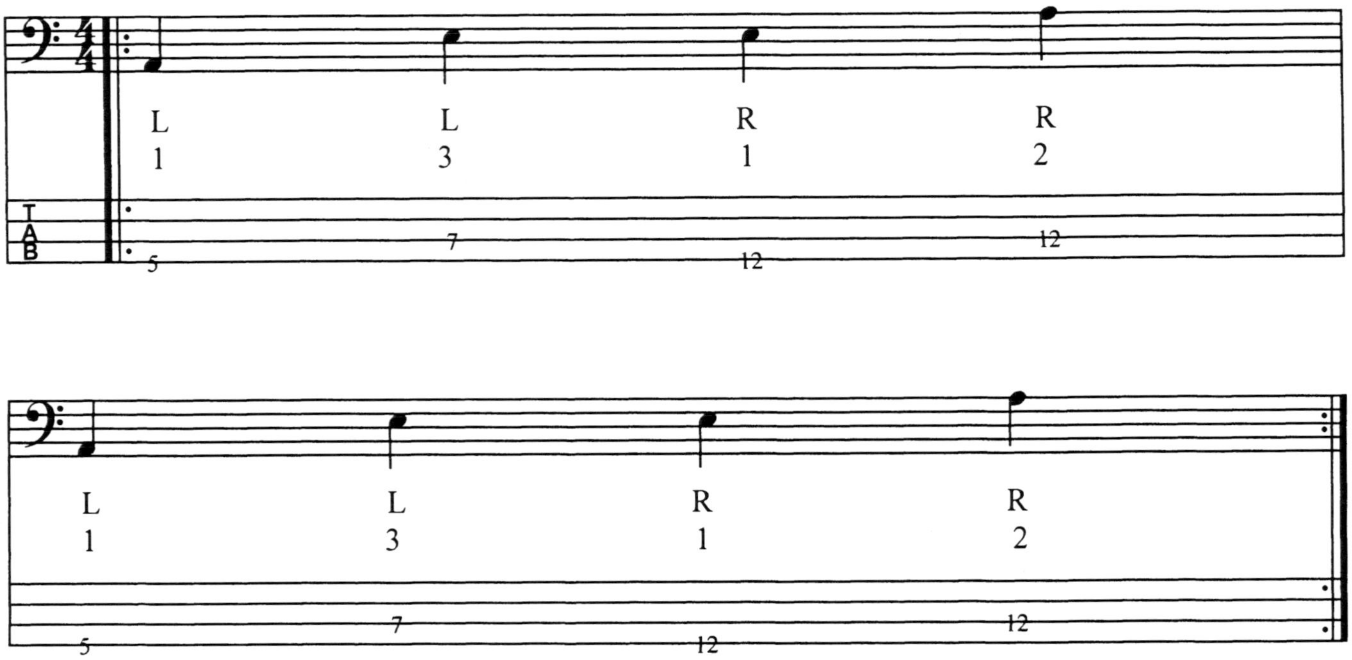

EXAMPLE 2:

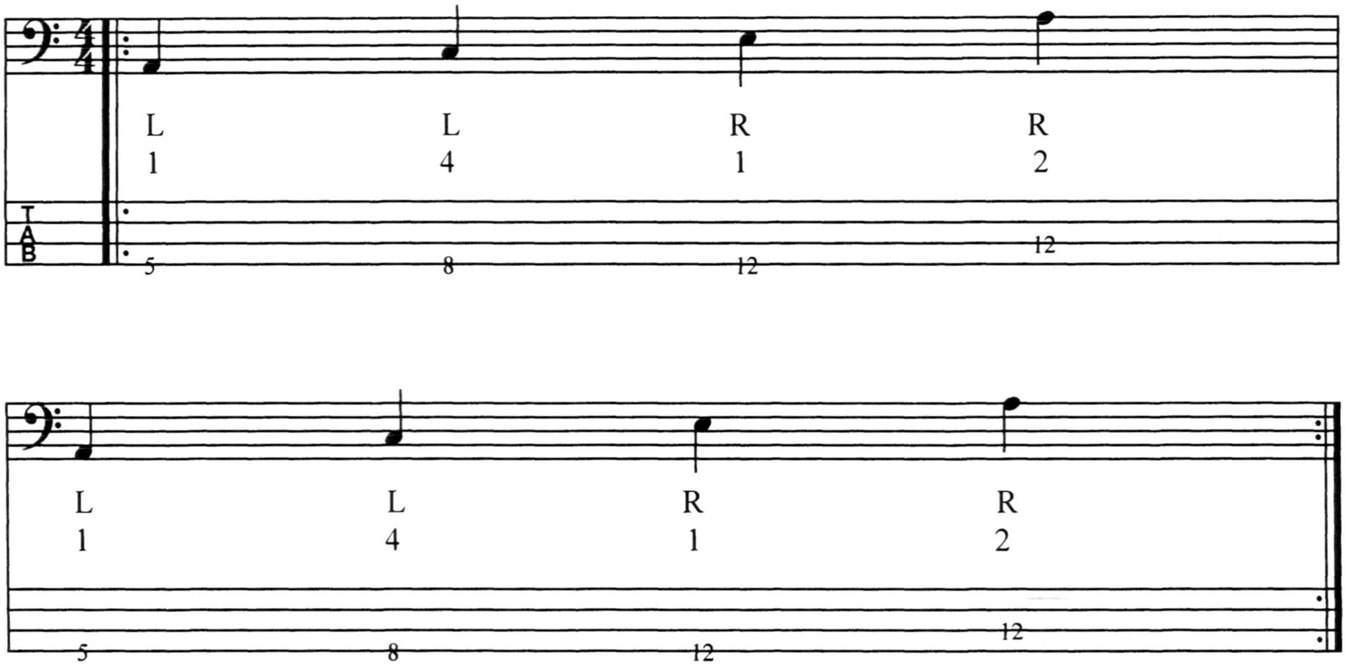

EXAMPLE 3:

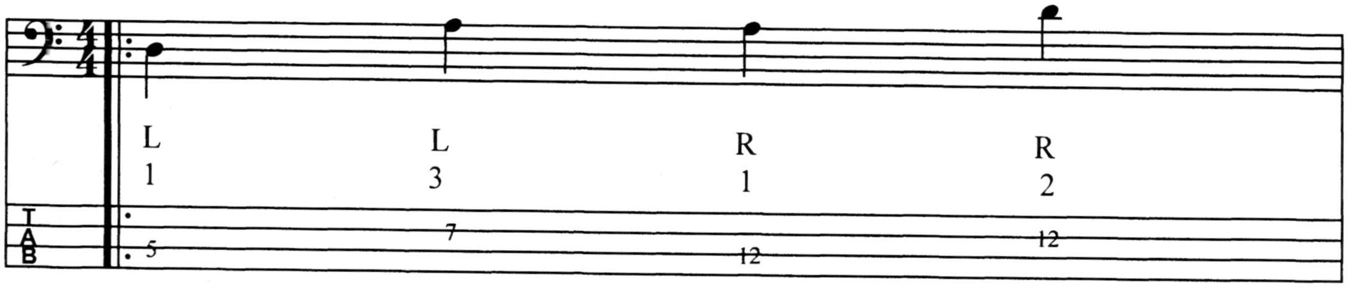

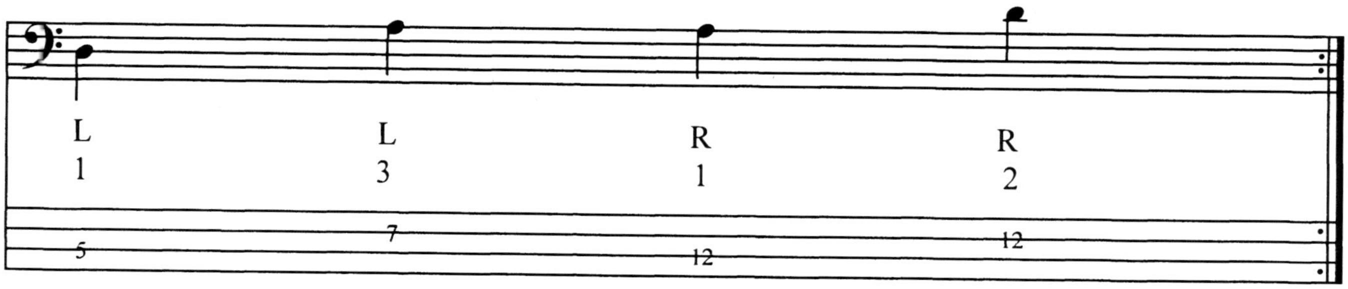

EXAMPLE 4:

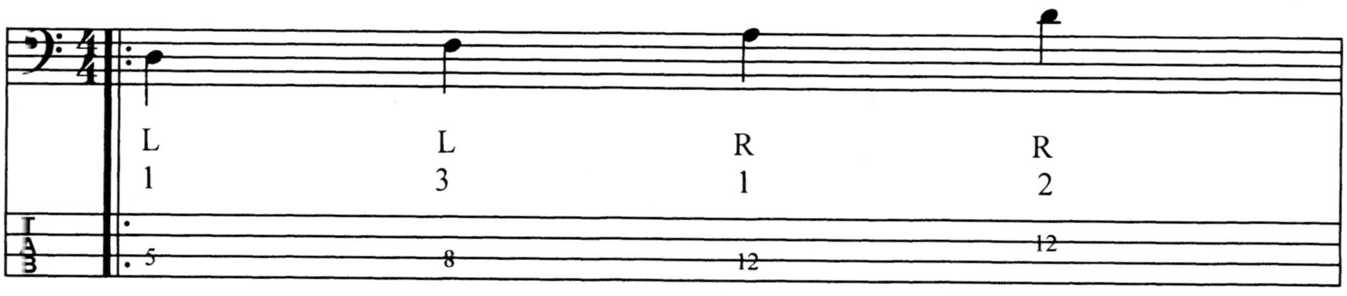

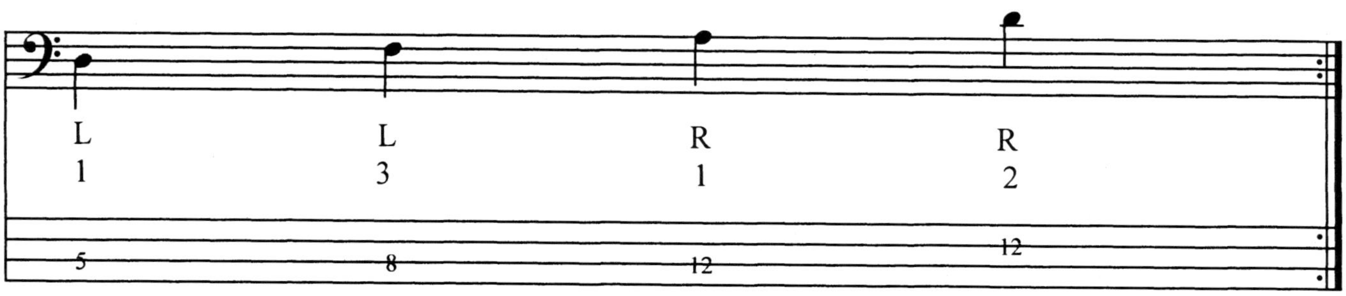

EXAMPLE 5:

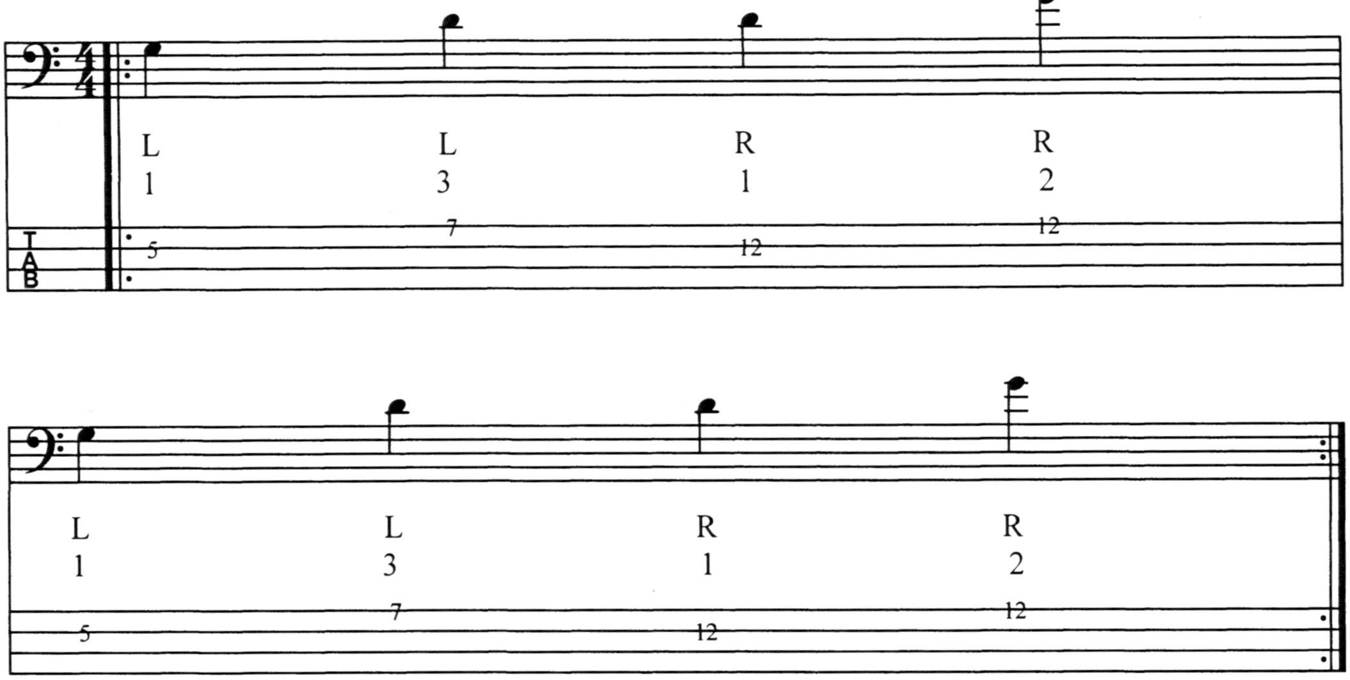

EXAMPLE 6:

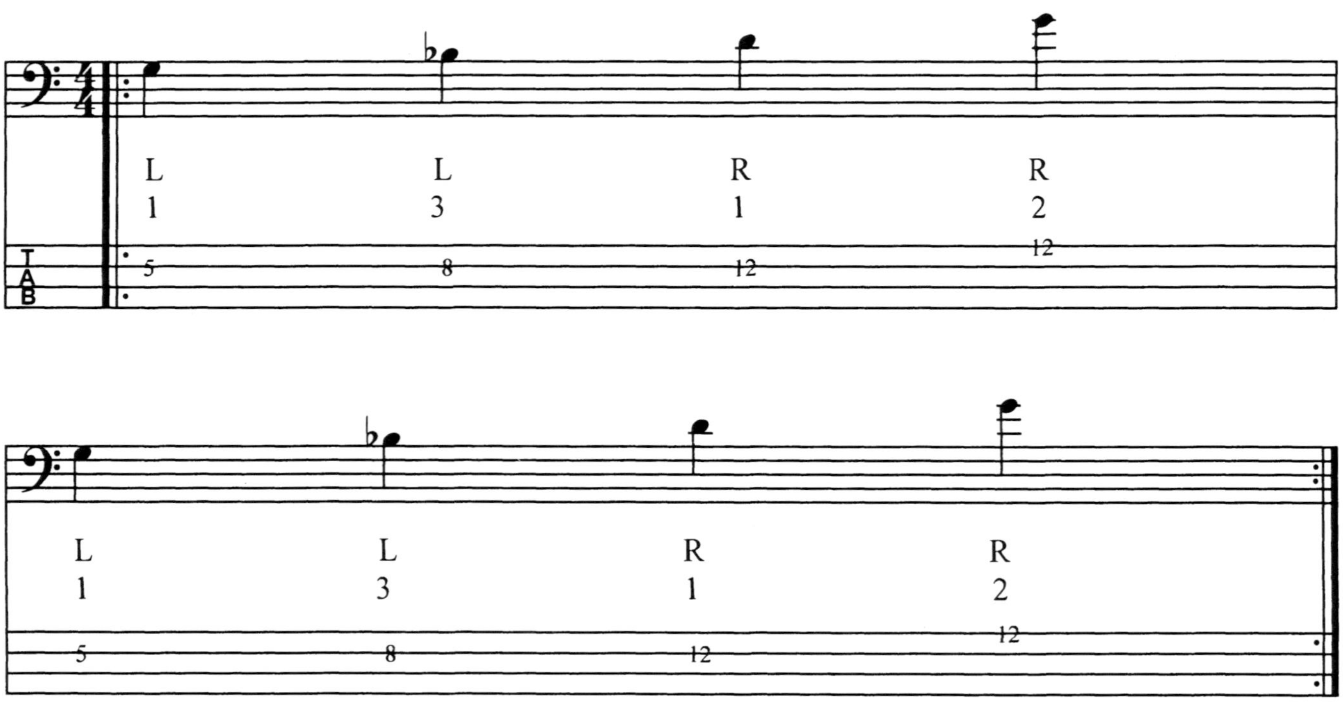

EXAMPLE 7:

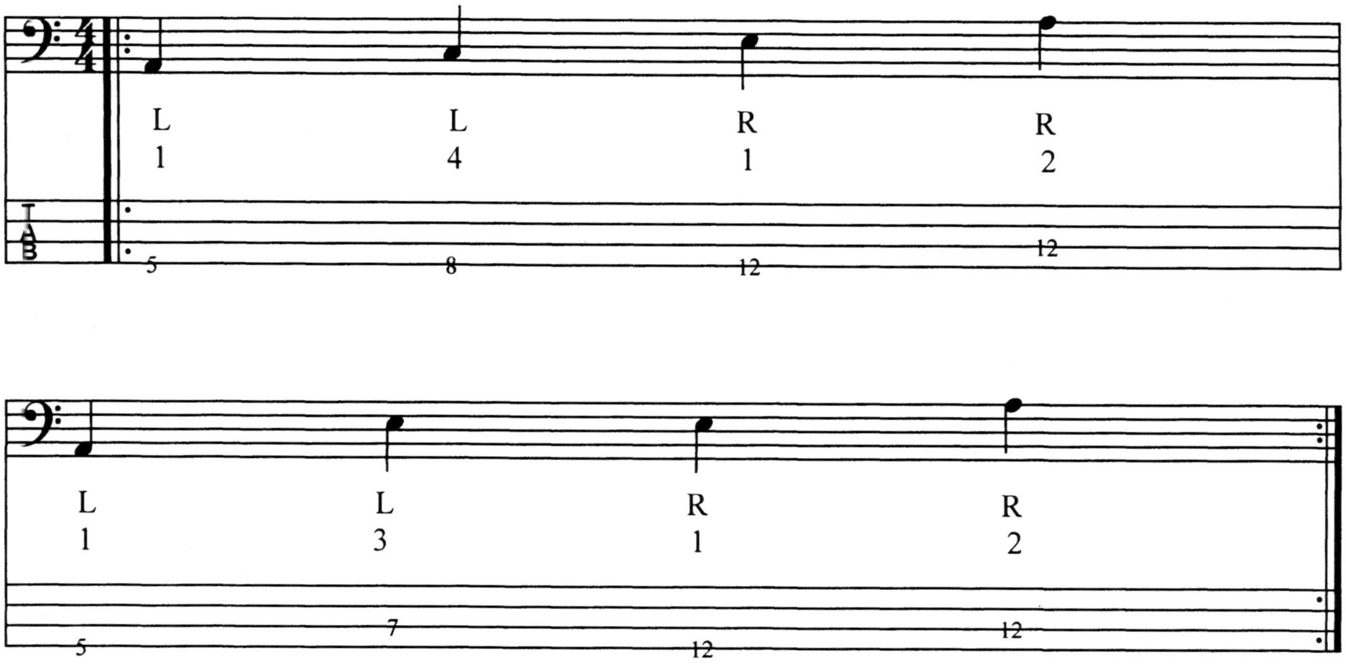

EXAMPLE 8:

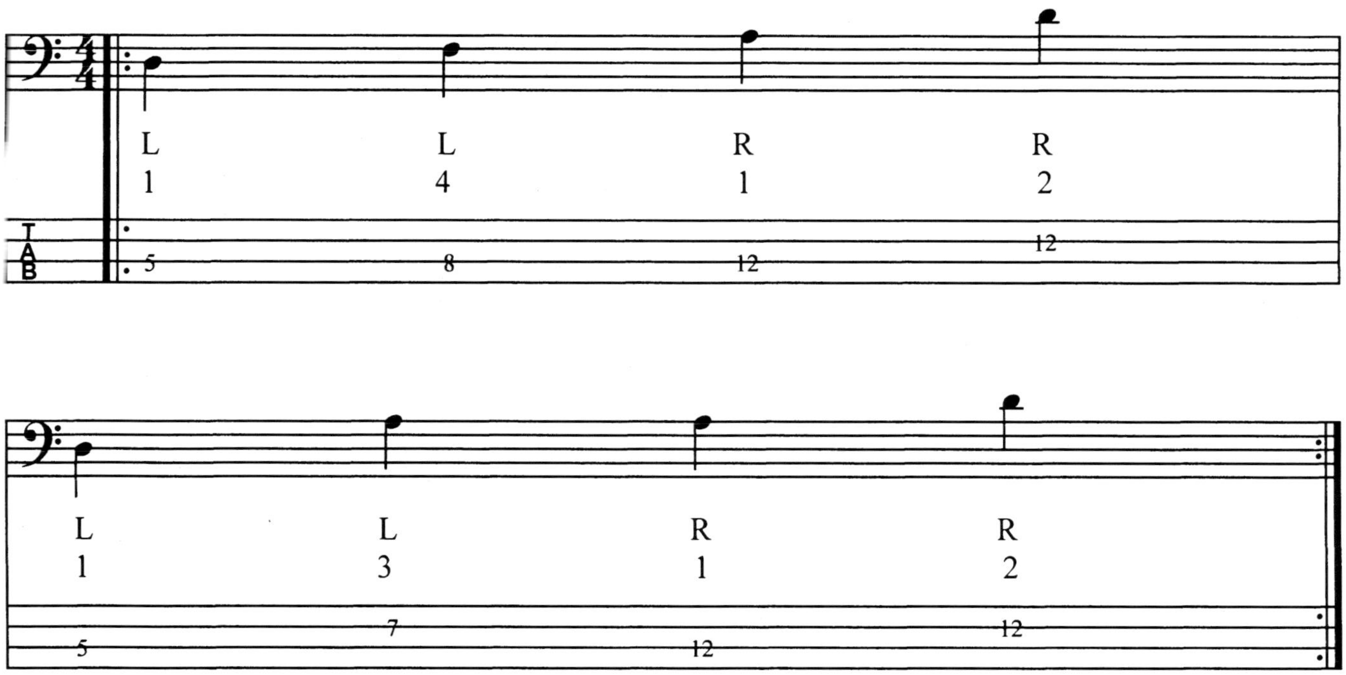

EXAMPLE 9:

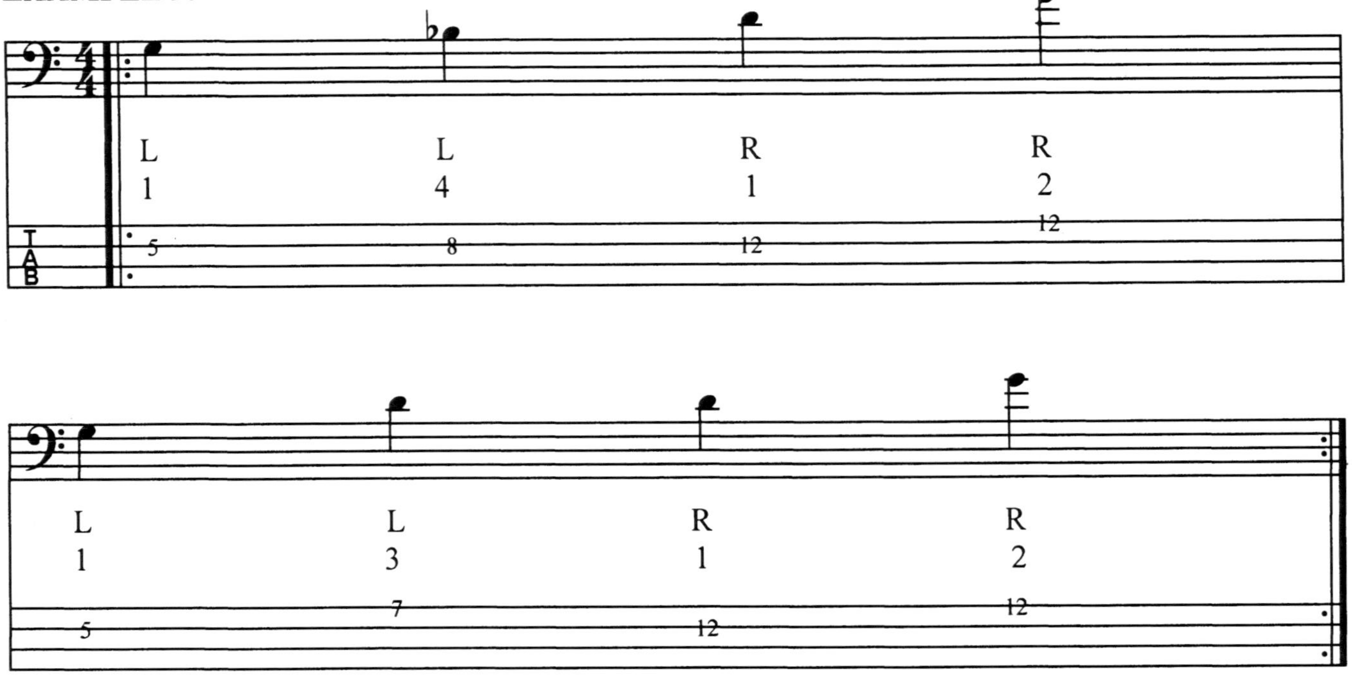

EXAMPLE 10:

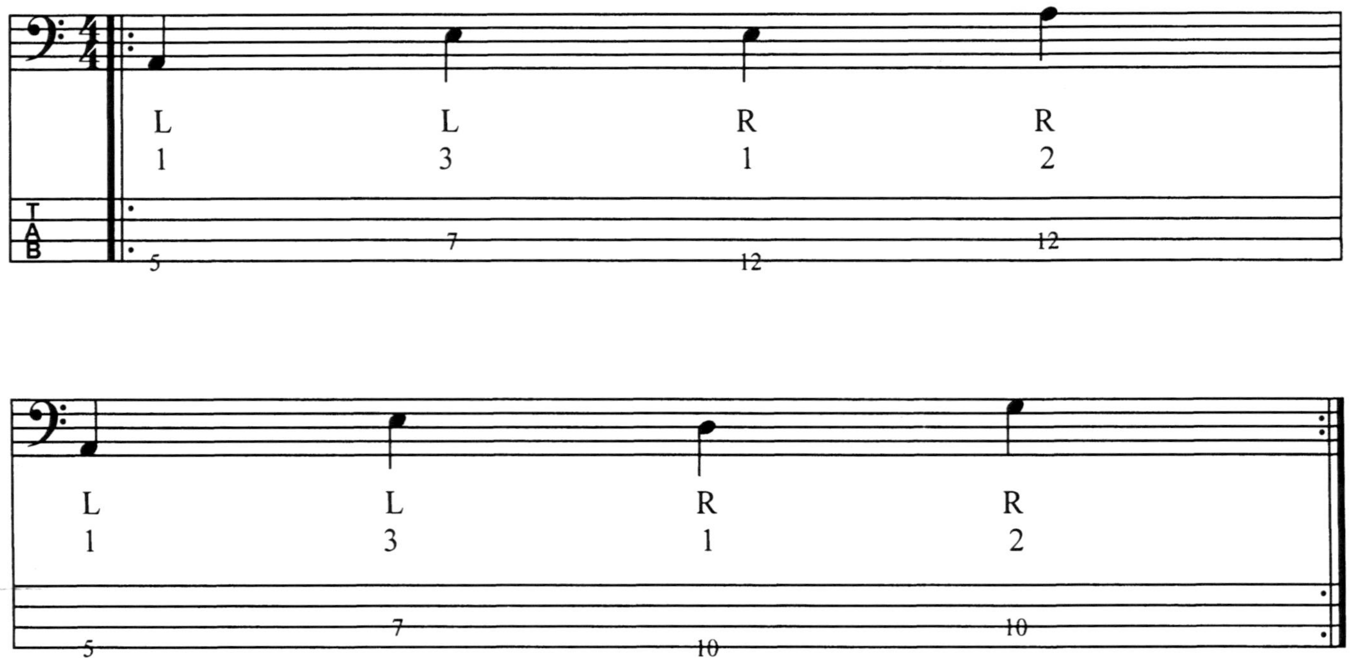

EXAMPLE 11:

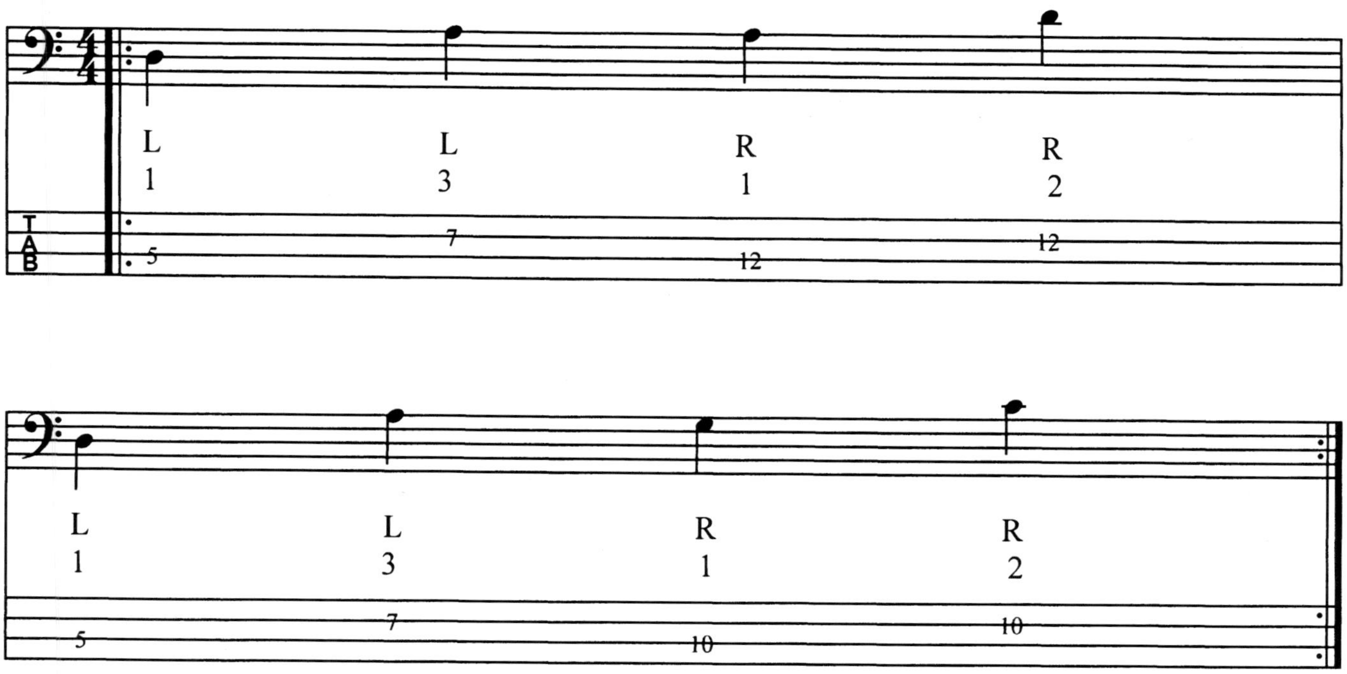

EXAMPLE 12:

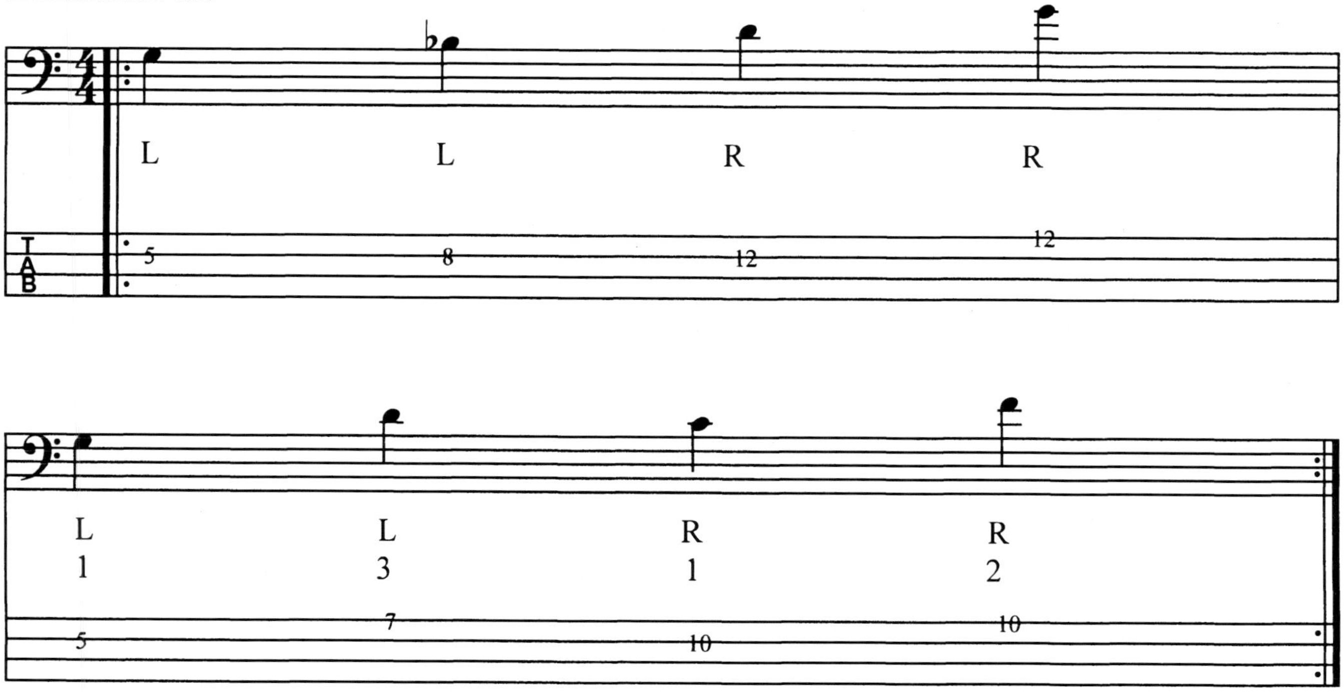

EXAMPLE 13:

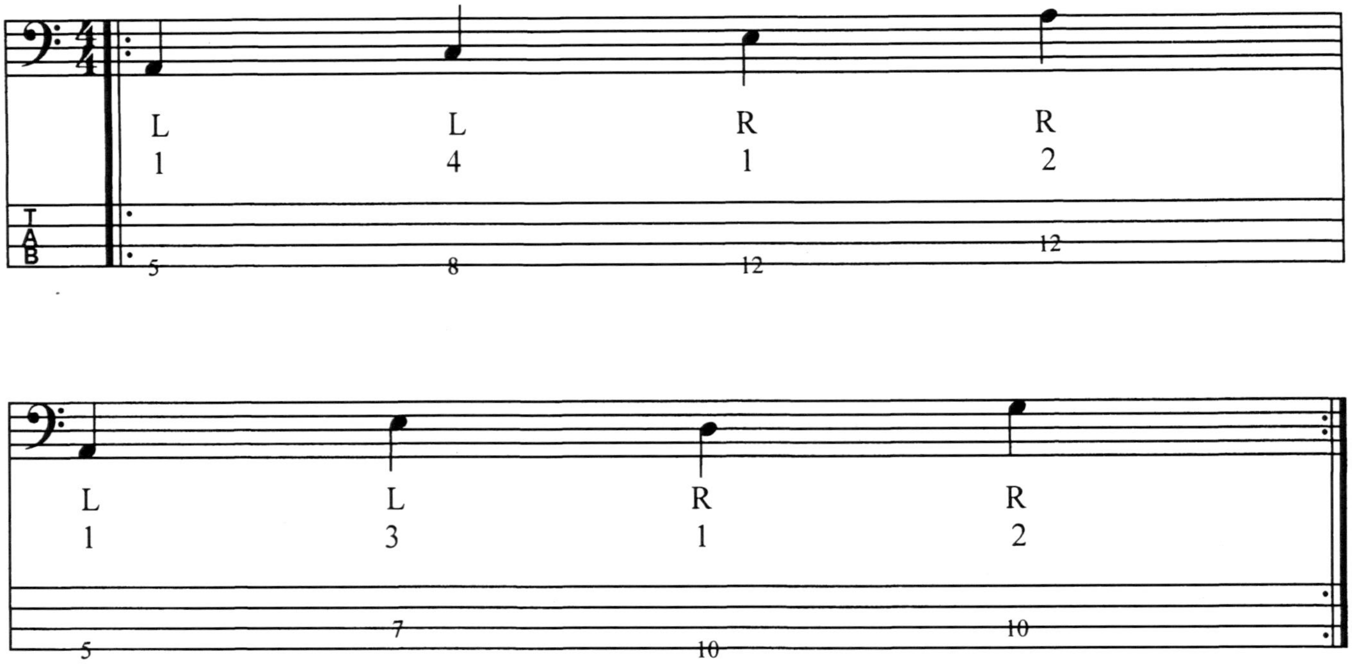

EXAMPLE 14:

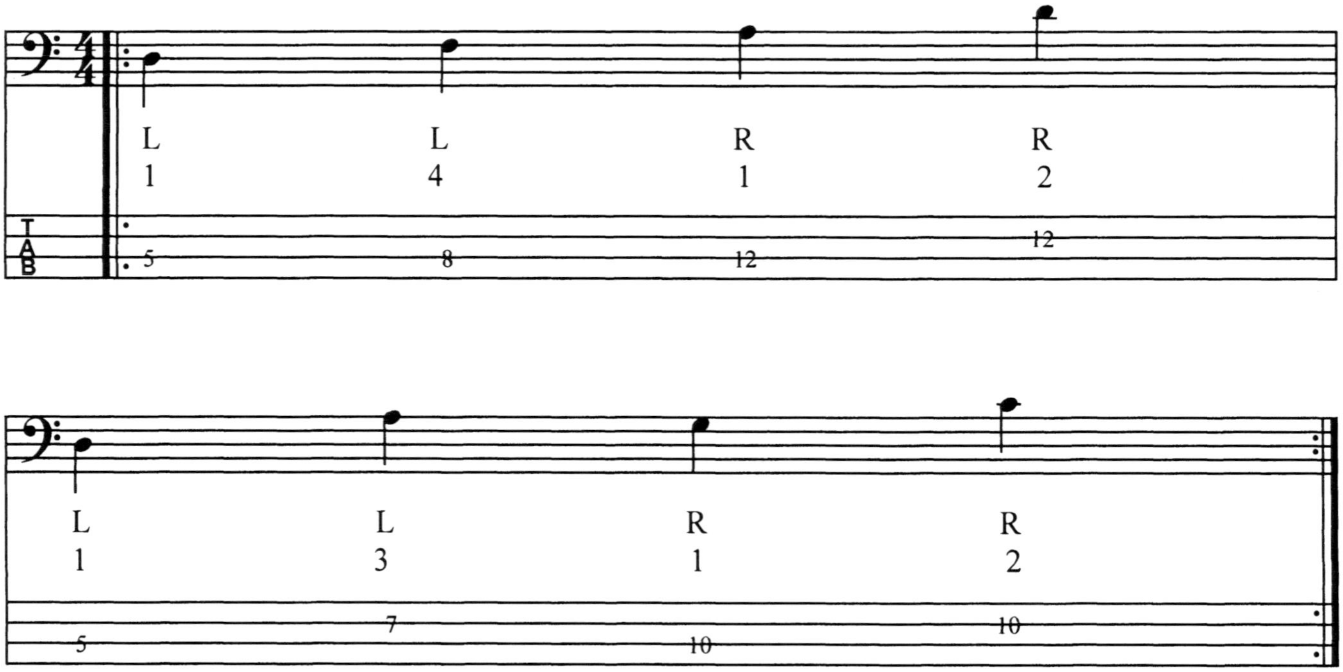

EXAMPLE 15:

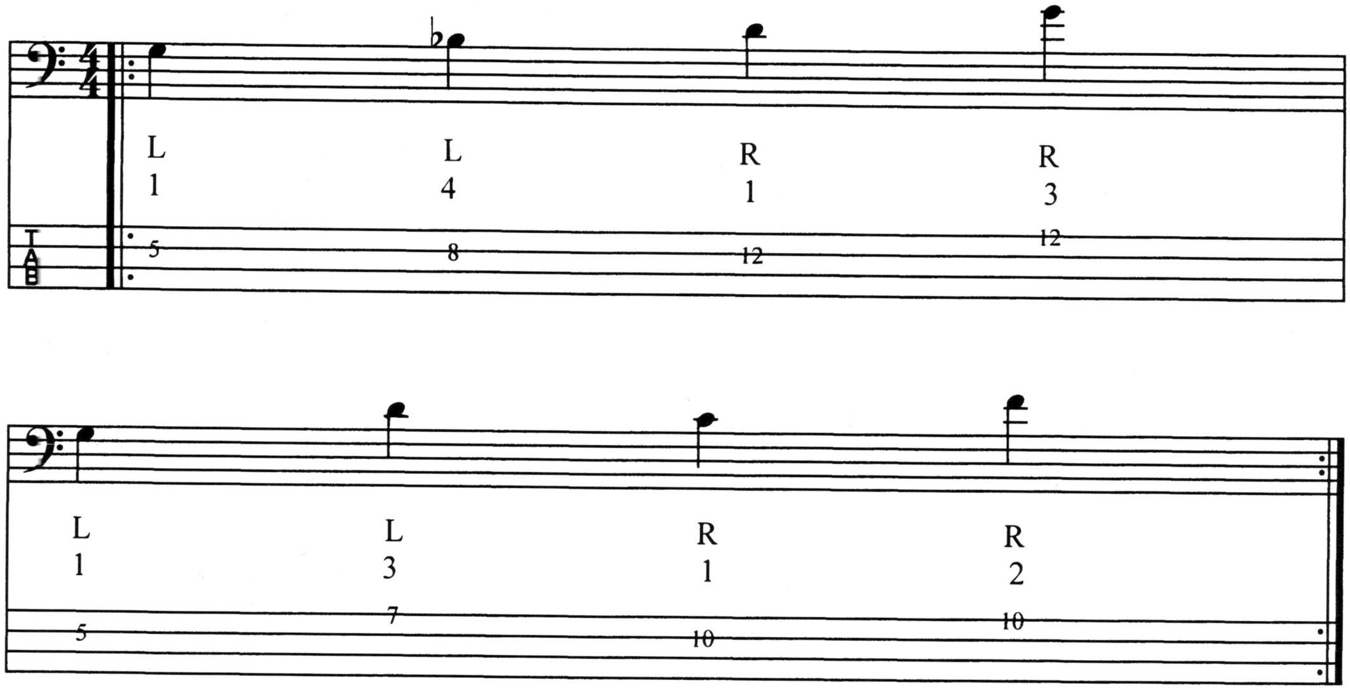

EXAMPLE 16:

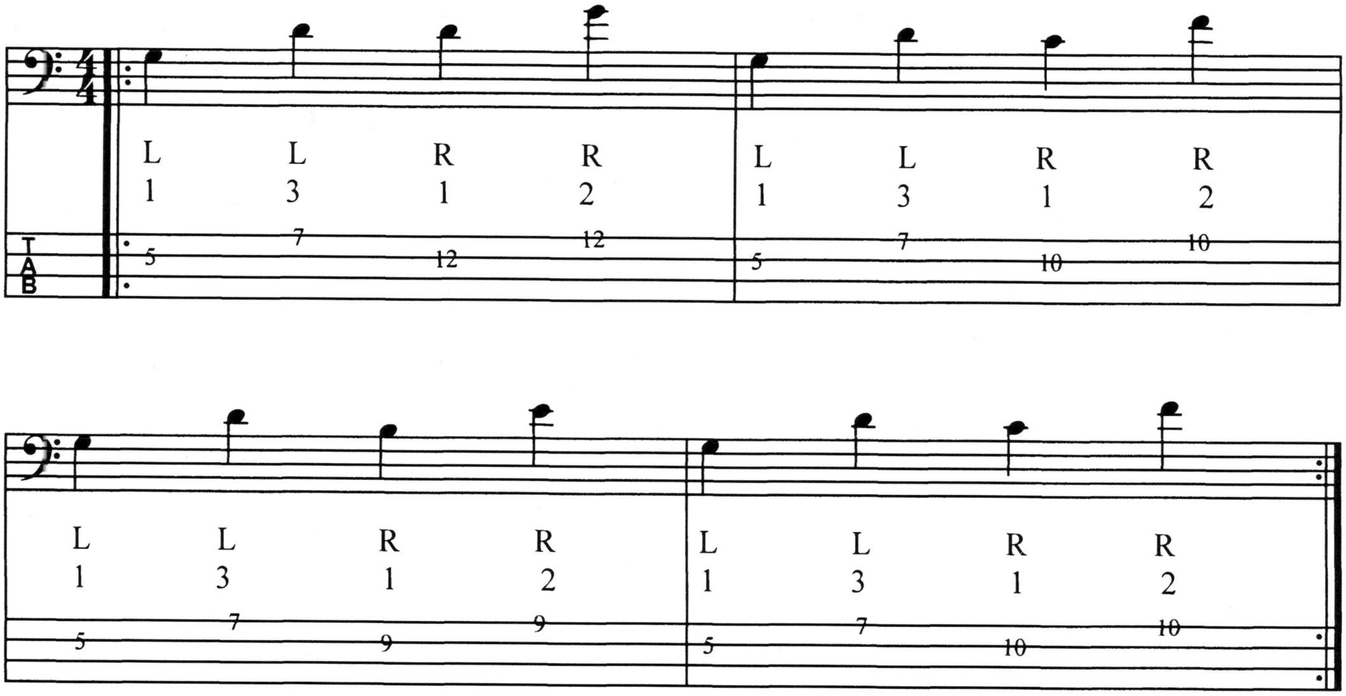

EXAMPLE 17:

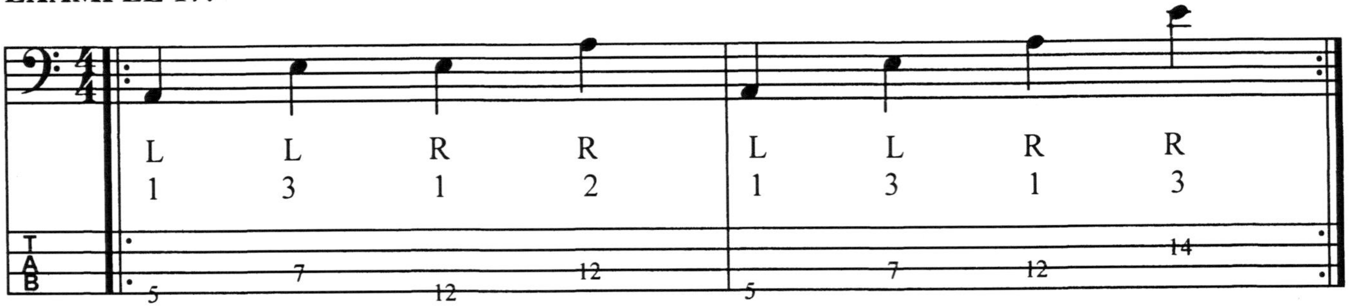

EXAMPLE 18:

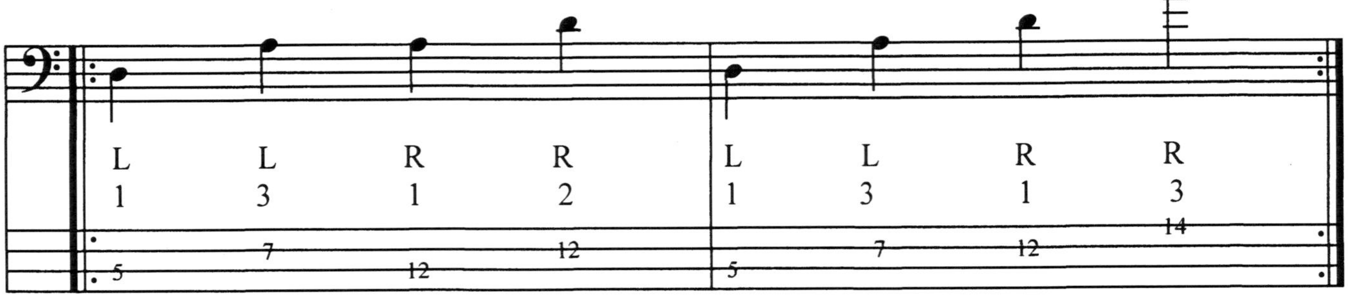

EXAMPLE 19:

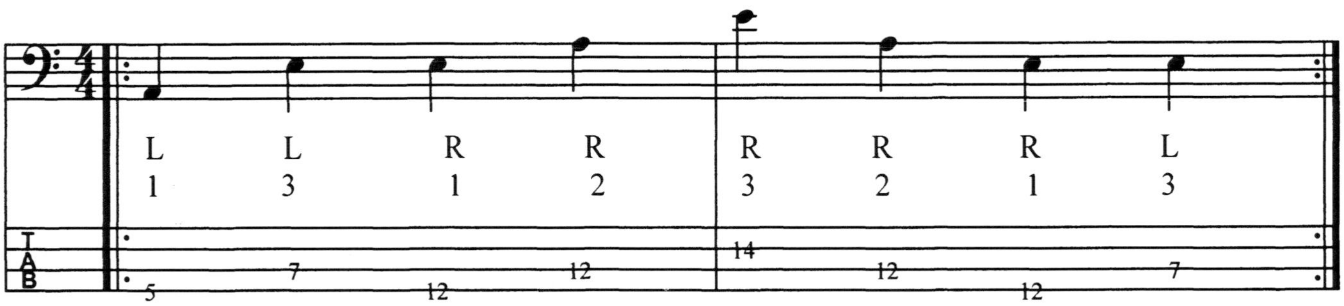

EXAMPLE 20:

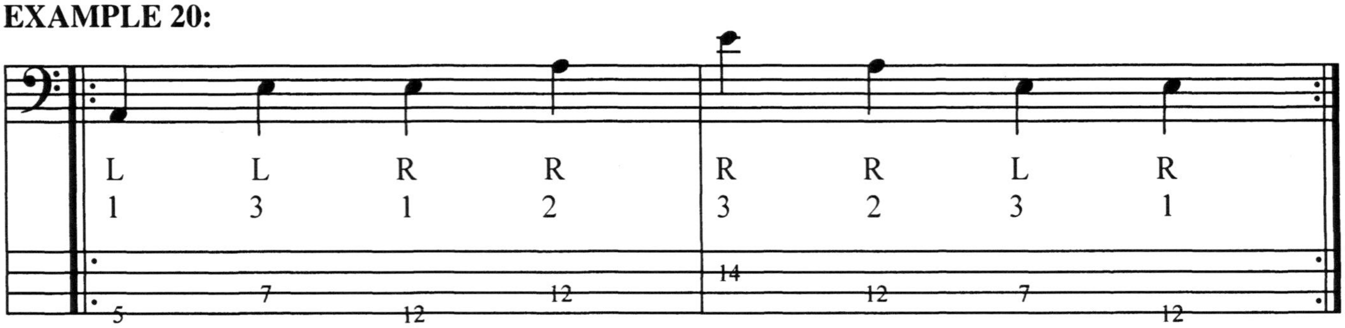

EXAMPLE 21:

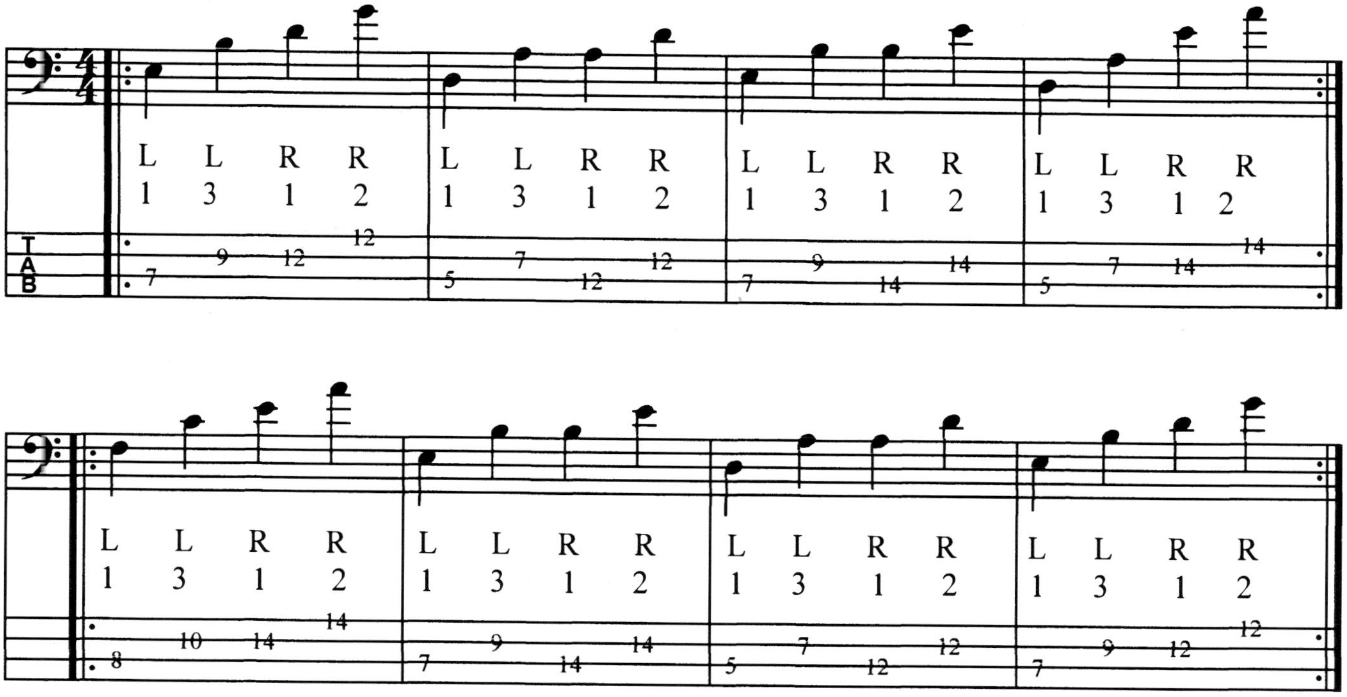

SCALES AND MODES

The following examples use some of the most common scales and modes in modern music. Each of the following examples plays scales in two octaves at once. The left hand plays all the notes below the seventh fret. The right hand plays all the notes above the seventh fret.

EXAMPLE 22: Major scale

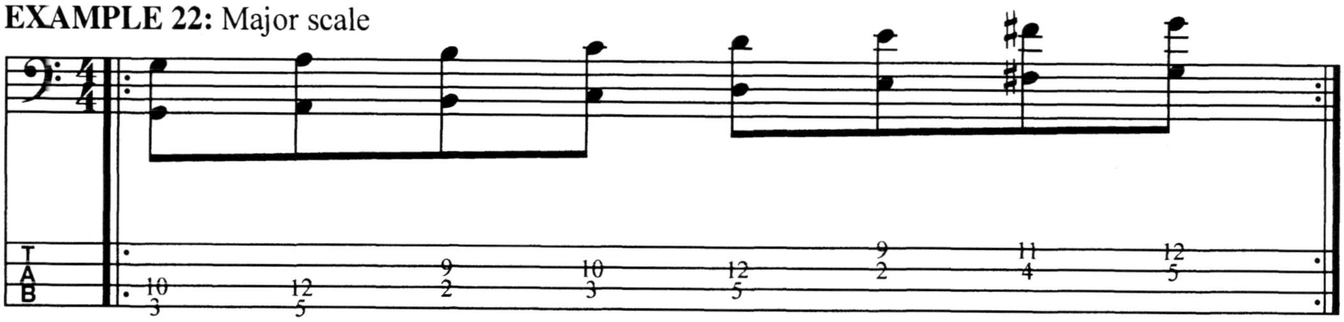

EXAMPLE 23: Minor scale

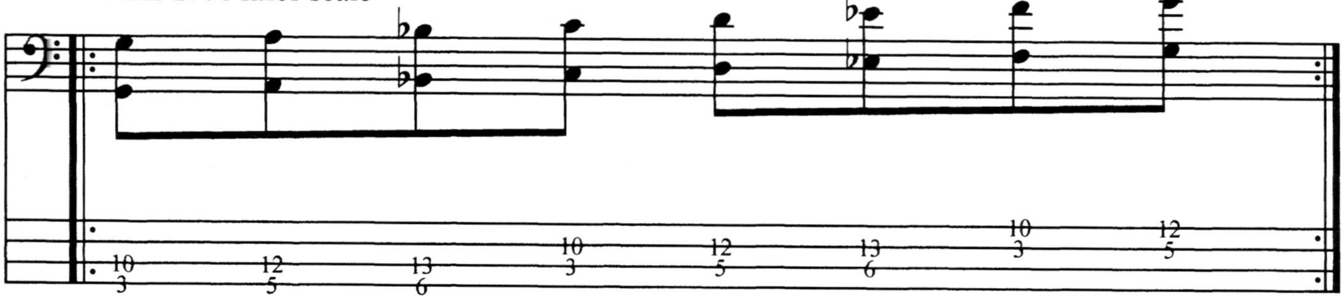

EXAMPLE 24: Mixolydian scale

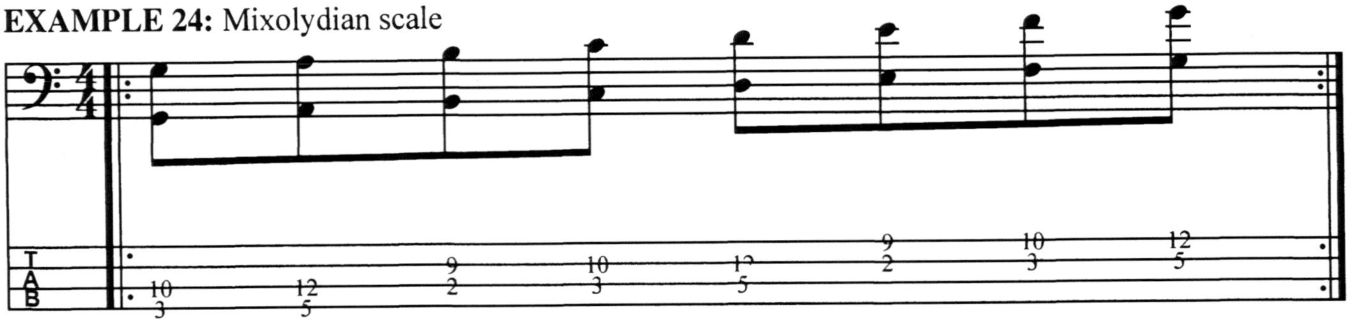

EXAMPLE 25: Major scale

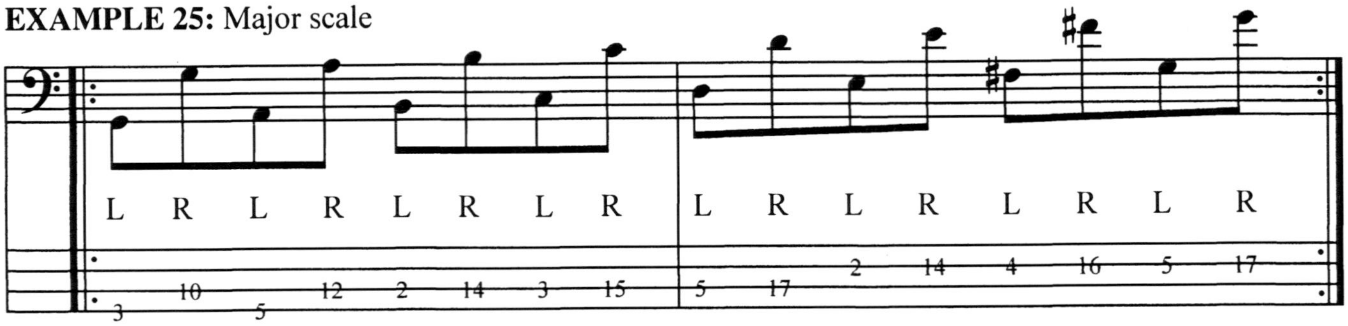

EXAMPLE 26: Minor scale

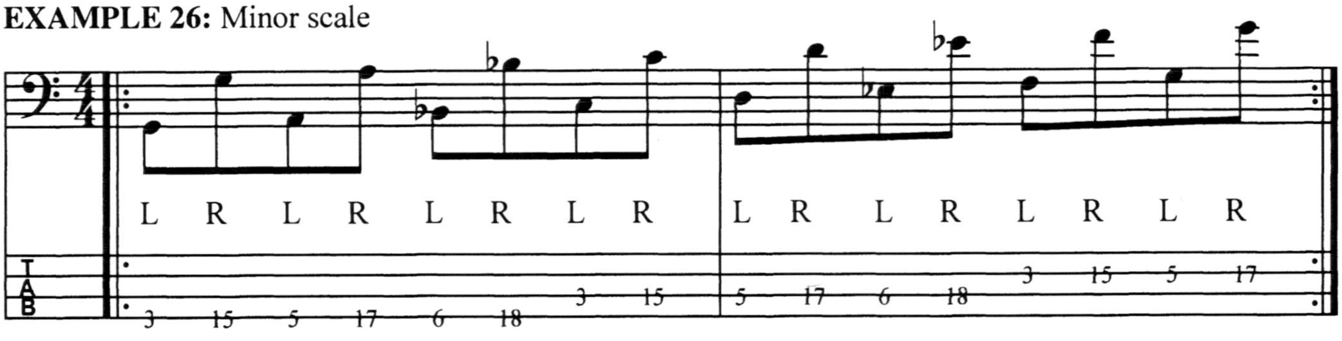

EXAMPLE 27: Mixolydian scale

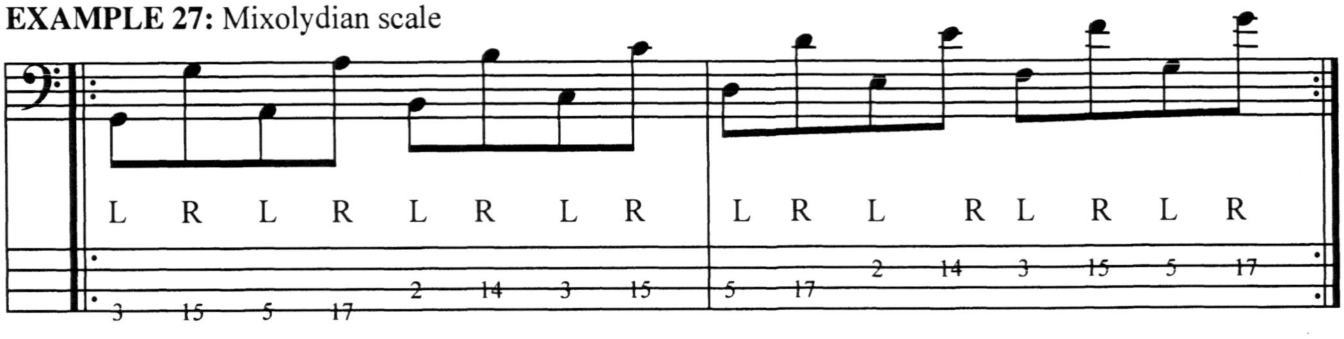

MODAL HARMONIZING

There are seven modes. Here they are in order in the key of C:

MAJOR	CDEFGABC
DORIAN	DEFGABCD
PHRYGIAN	EFGABCDE
LYDIAN	FGABCDEF
MIXOLYDIAN	GABCDEFG
AOLIAN(minor)	ABCDEFGA
LOCRIAN	BCDEFGAB

Pick a mode and play it with your left hand only. For example try playing Aolian starting on your fifth fret E string. Now go down the mode list two modes from Aolian. That would put you back to the top of the list at Major. Tap the Major scale in the high register of your bass with your right hand.

EXAMPLE 28: Now try them together.

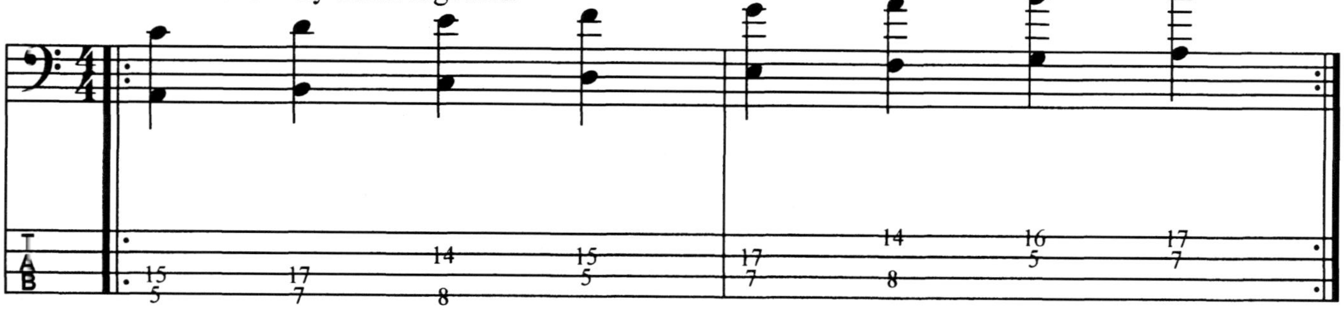

EXAMPLE 29: G Mixolydian in the left hand and B Locrian in the right hand.

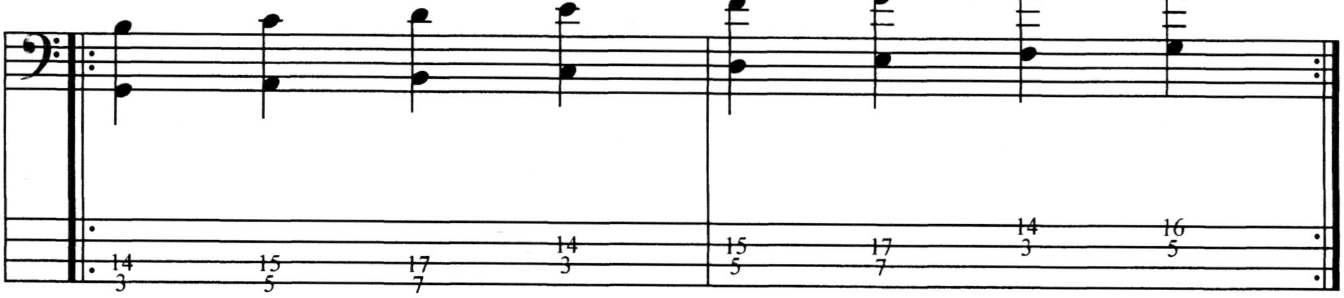

The last two examples were in the key of C. The key of C has no sharps or flats. Two-hand tapping in other keys will require some knowledge of the circle of fifths. The circle of fifths will tell you what notes to play sharp or flat.

EXAMPLE 30: This example is in the key of G. The key of G has one sharp (f). Play all F's sharp. The left hand plays the Phrygian scale. The right hand plays the Mixolydian scale.

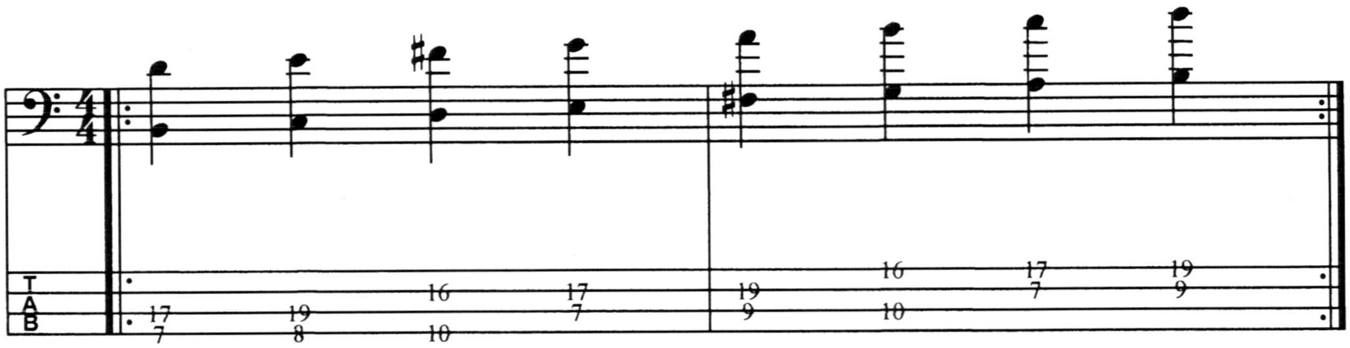

There are many modal combinations. Try exploring different keys. If the circle of fifths seems confusing then you may want to work with a qualified teacher...

DIMINISHED PATTERN

Tapping with diminished patterns can create some interesting sounding textures.

EXAMPLE 31: Both hands play notes at the same time. The right hand plays the low pitched notes.

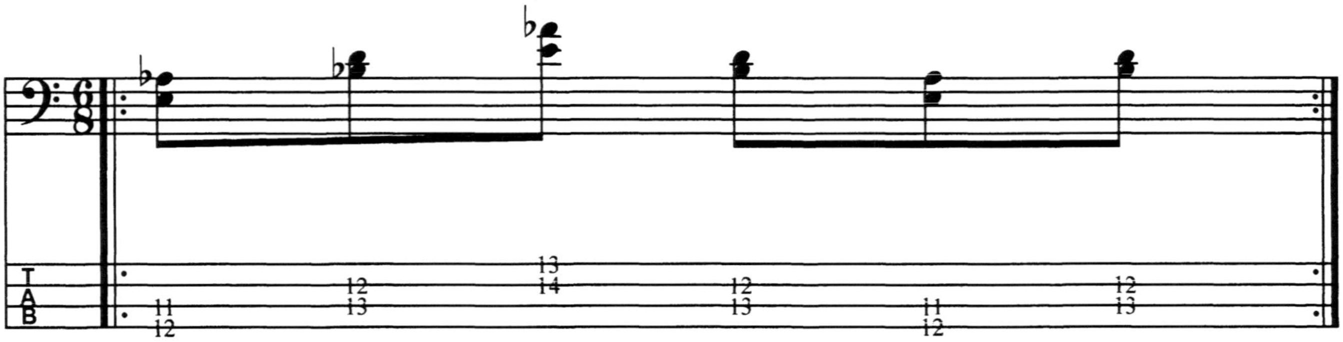

EXAMPLE 32:

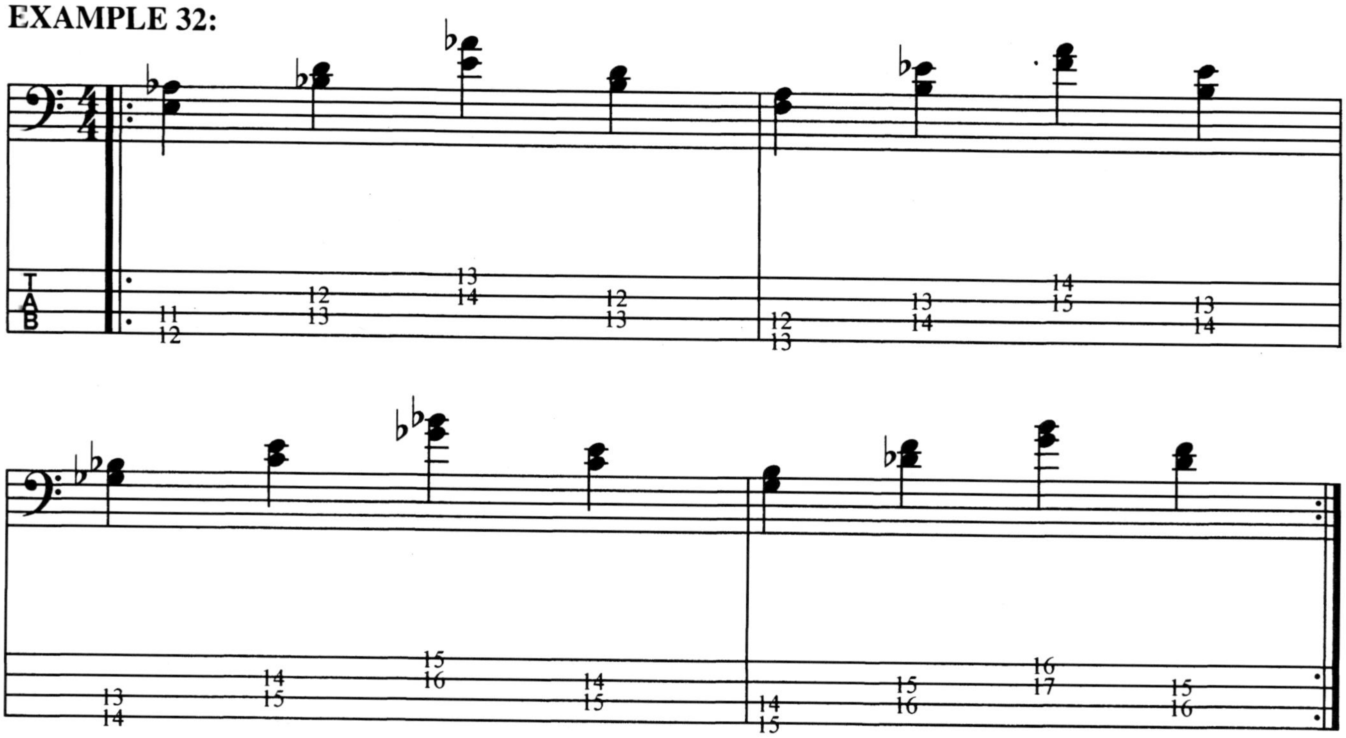

SCALES WITH HAMMERS

EXAMPLE 33: The left hand plays a double hammer pattern on the E string. The right hand traces a Major scale in twelfth position.

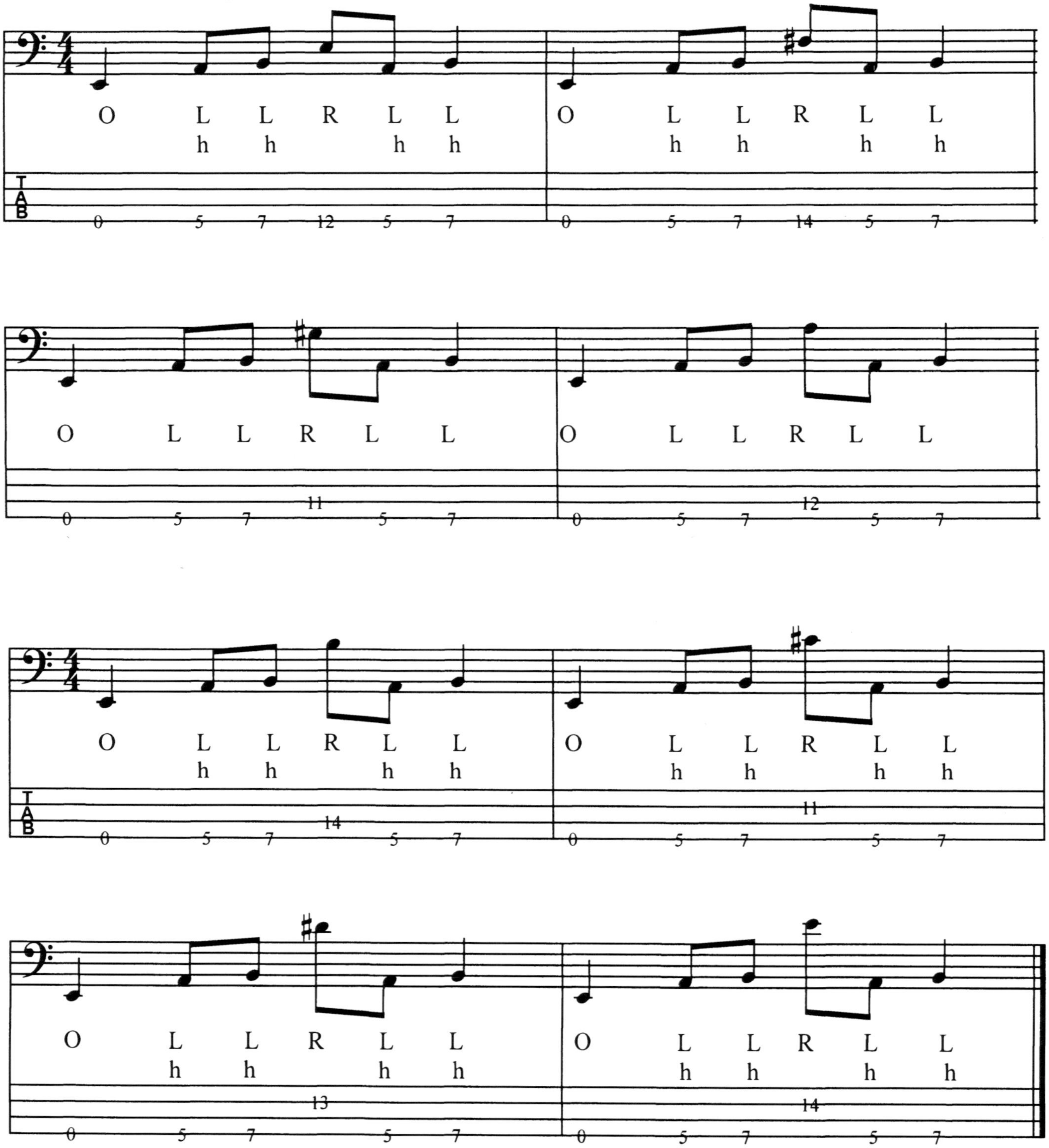

EXAMPLE 34: The right hand traces a Minor scale in twelfth position.

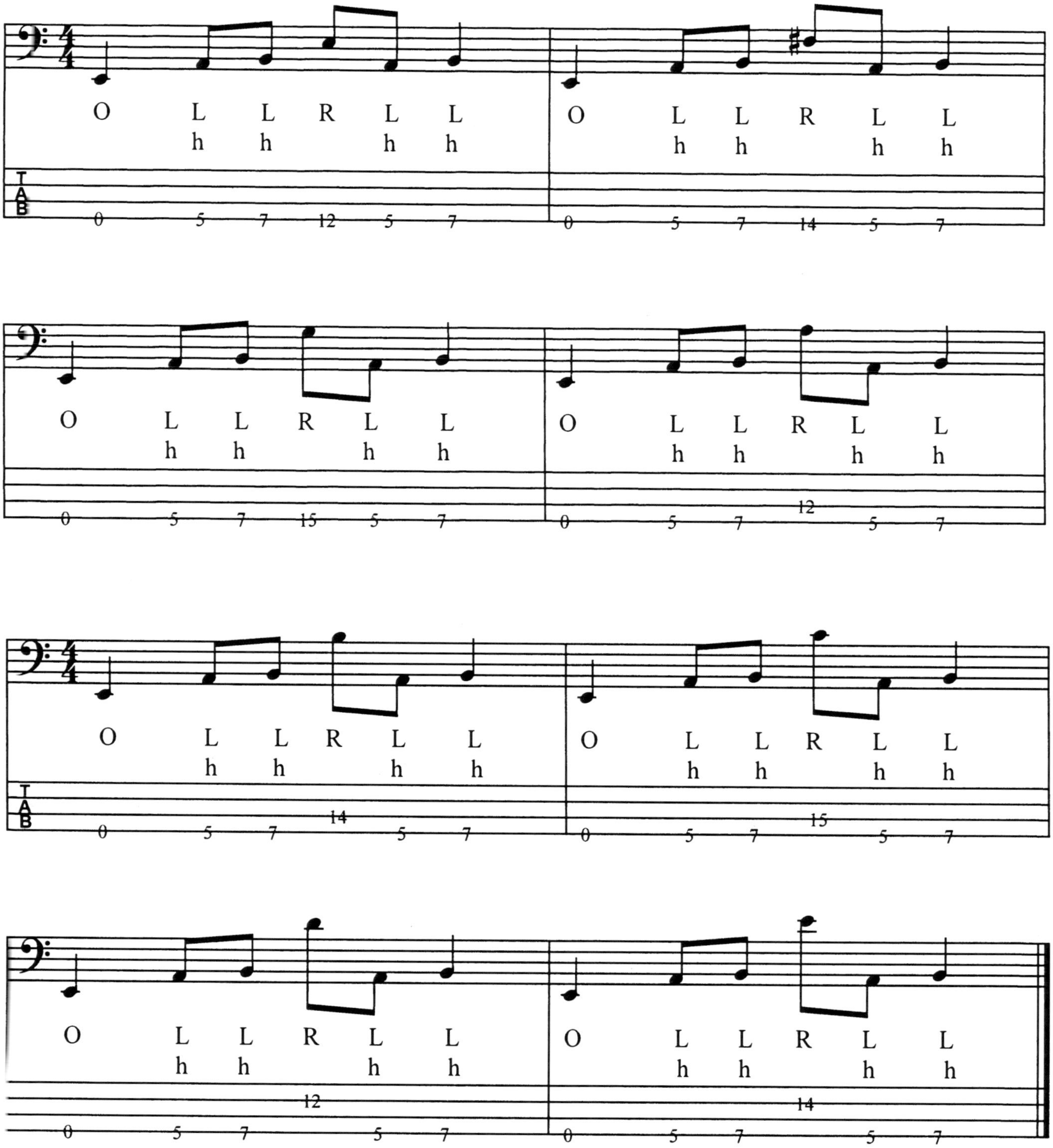

NOTE: In the last two exercises the first note can be struck in a few ways. I play it with my right hand thumb. It can be plucked or slapped. You can also play it with the fingers of your right hand with a standard fingerstyle approach.

Try exploring other scales with this technique. You can also explore notes beyond the octave in the right hand.

SETTING UP YOUR BASS FOR TAPPING: Low action makes tapping simpler. The lower the action, the less work your hands have to do. Some bassists like to use light strings when tapping. Short scale basses are also very popular for tapping.
REVERB: Different reverb settings can enhance your tapping. You may want to explore some Reverb units when tapping.
OTHER EFFECTS: Some bassists use exciters and compressers when tapping. Both effects can smooth out your signal.

TAPPING WITH CHORDS

There are many types of chords. The chords below are some of the most commonly found chords in modern music. The left hand plays notes on the E and A strings. The right hand plays notes on the D and G strings.

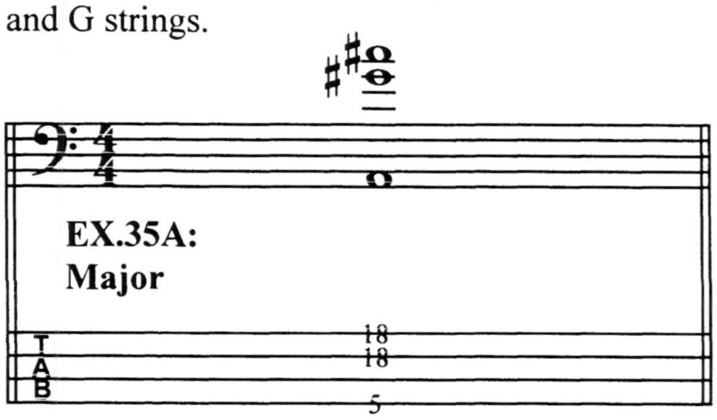

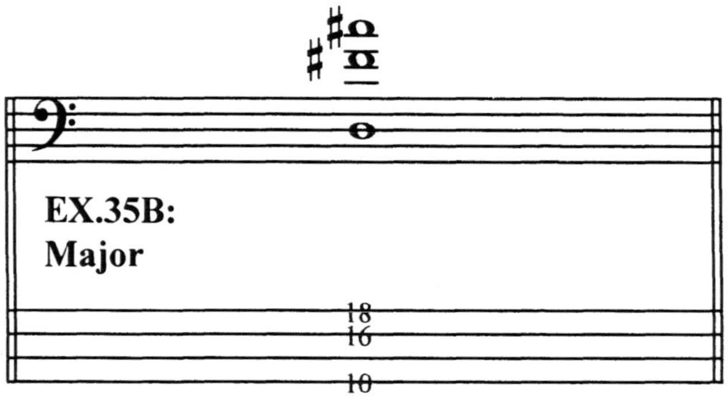

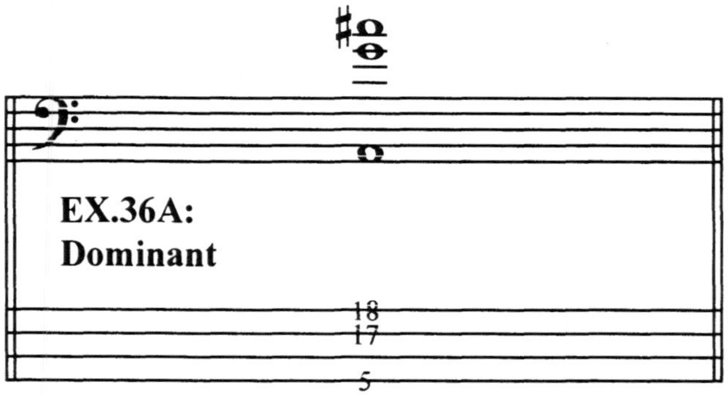

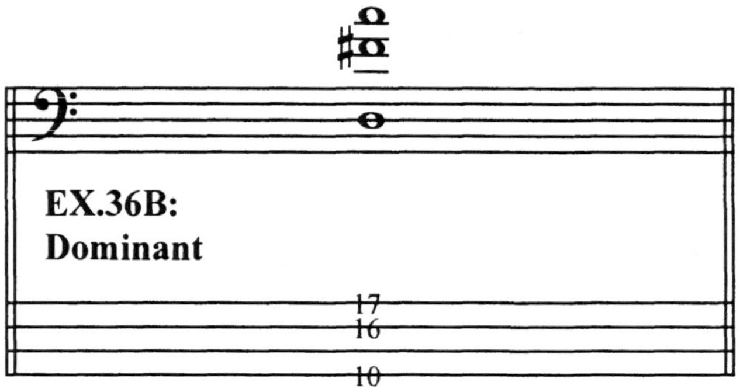

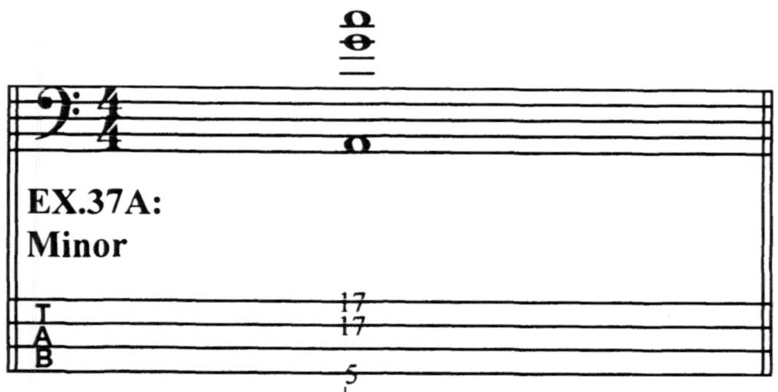

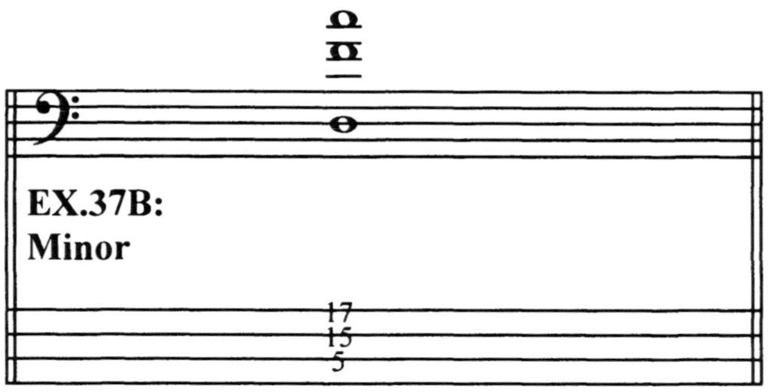

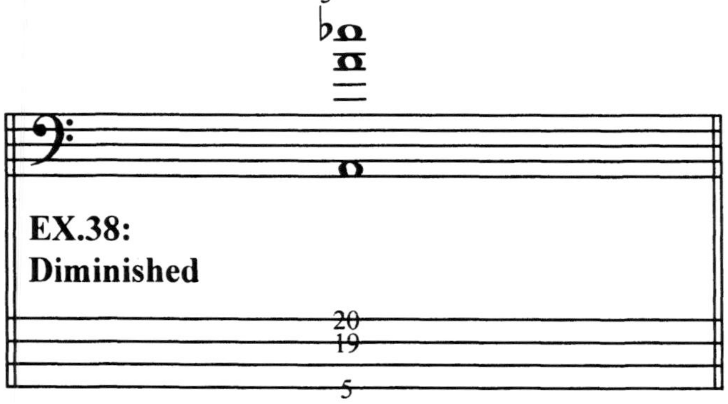

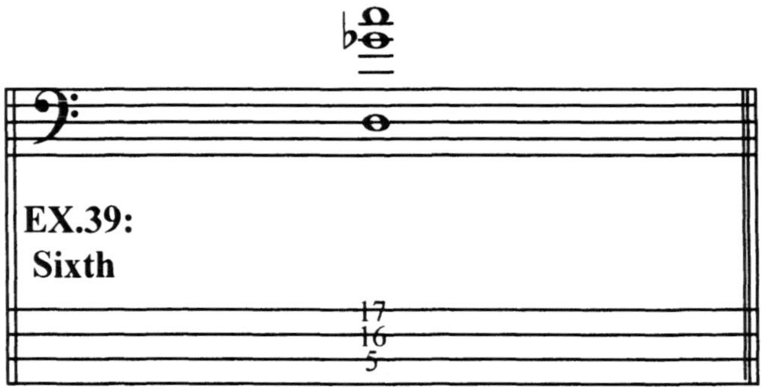

EXAMPLE 40:

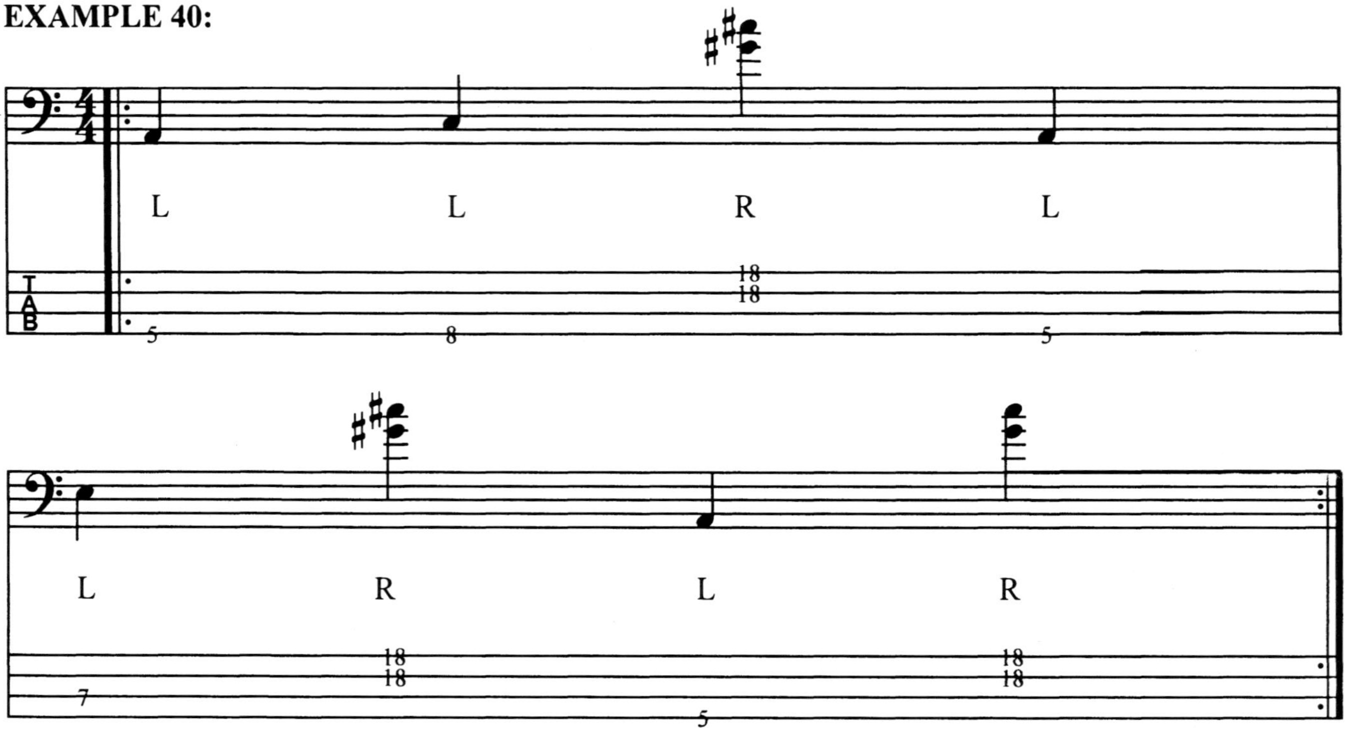

EXAMPLE 41:

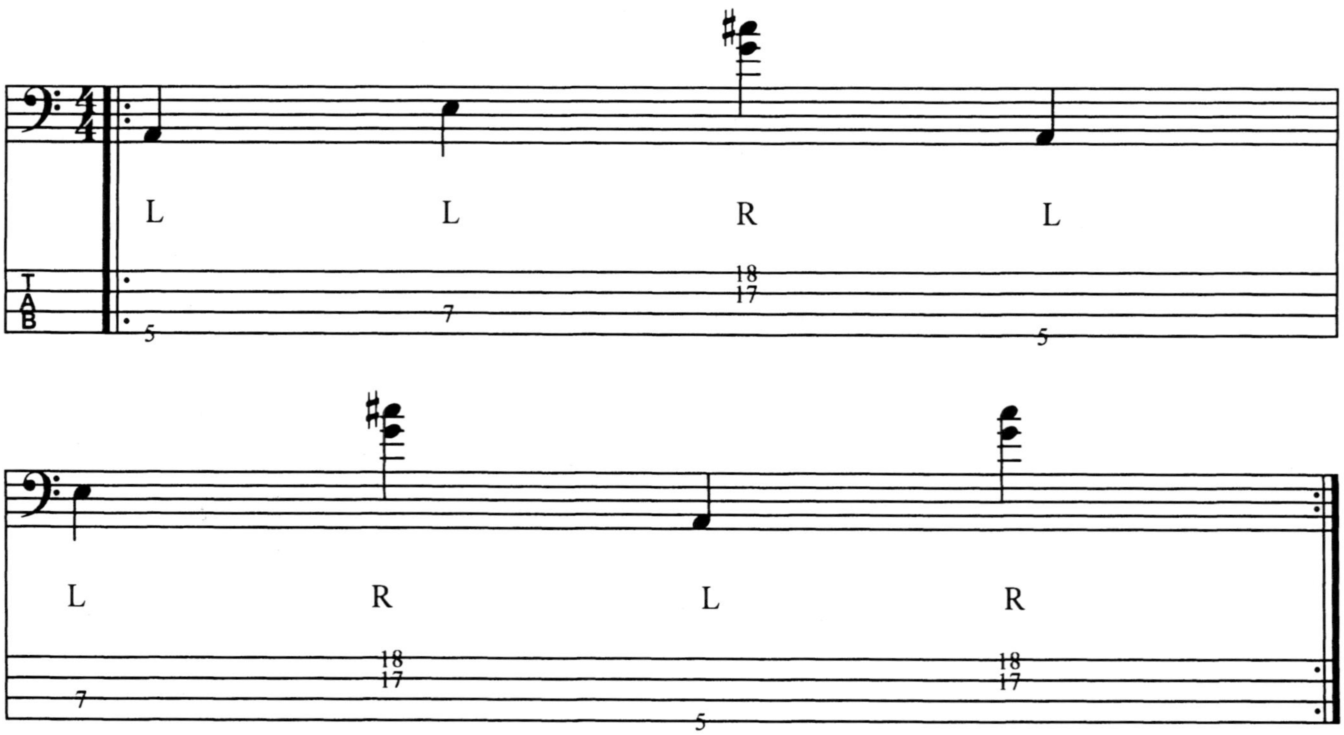

EXAMPLE 42:

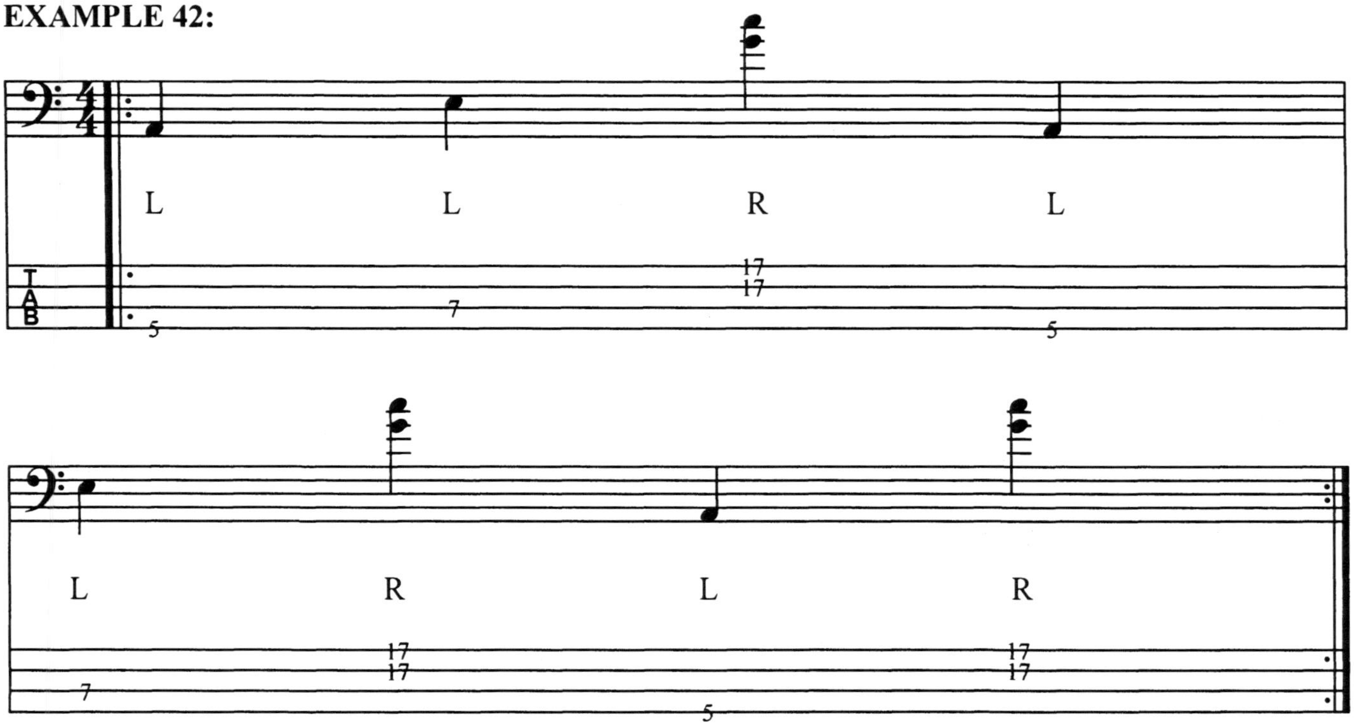

EXAMPLE 43:

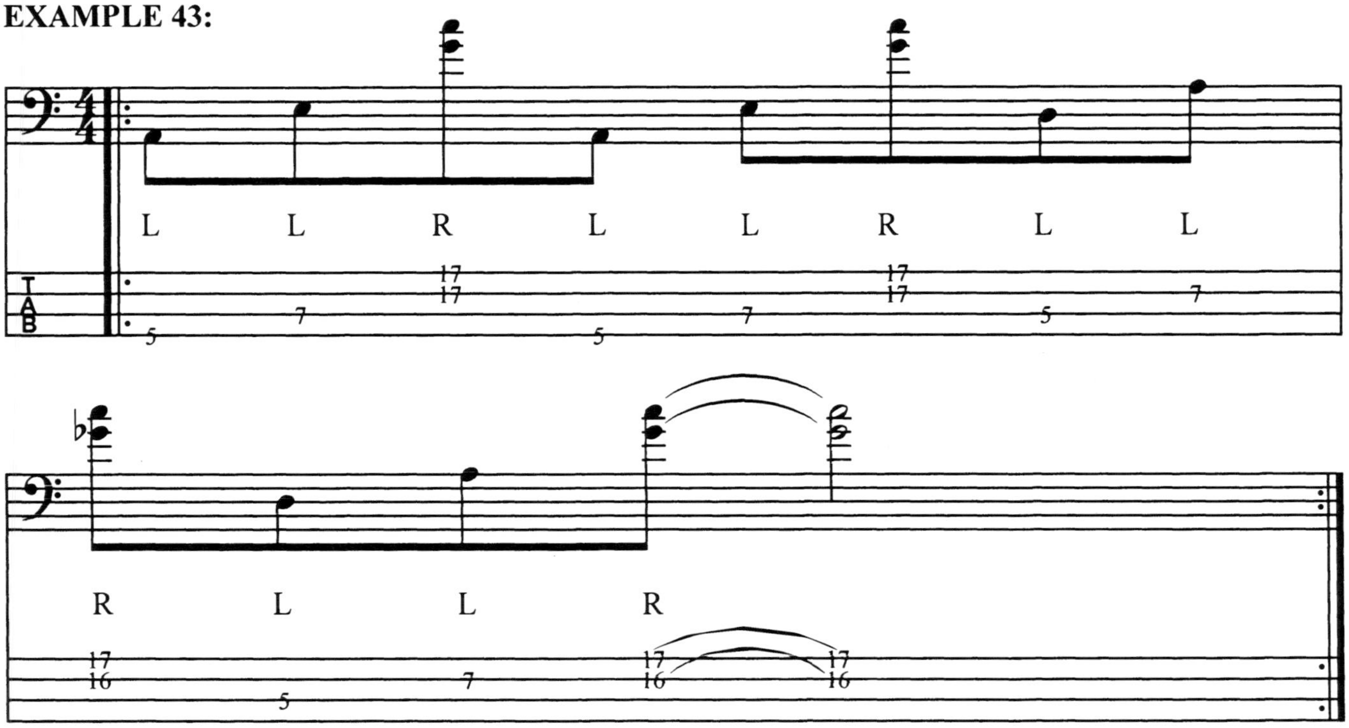

EXAMPLE 44:

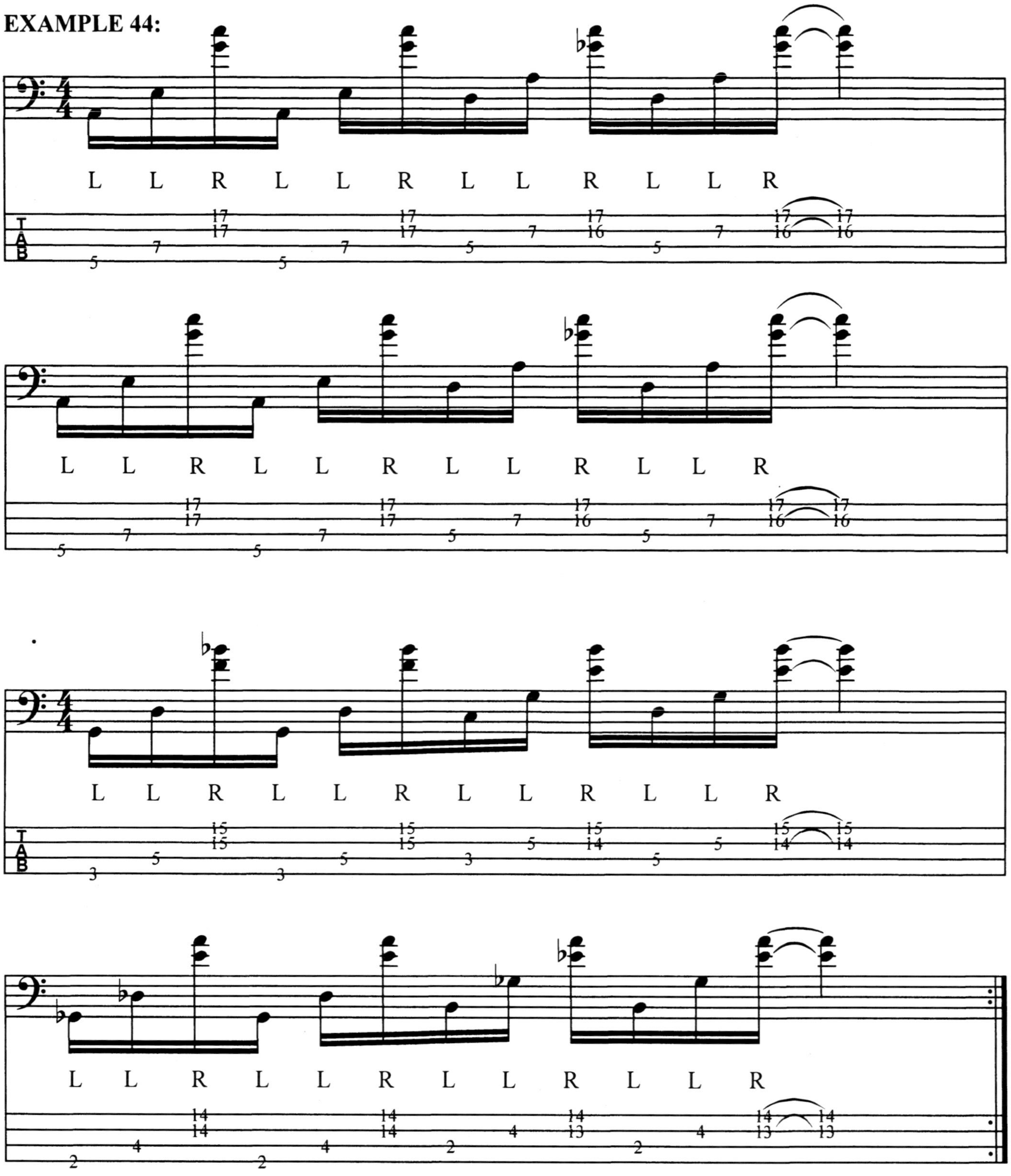

EXAMPLE 45:

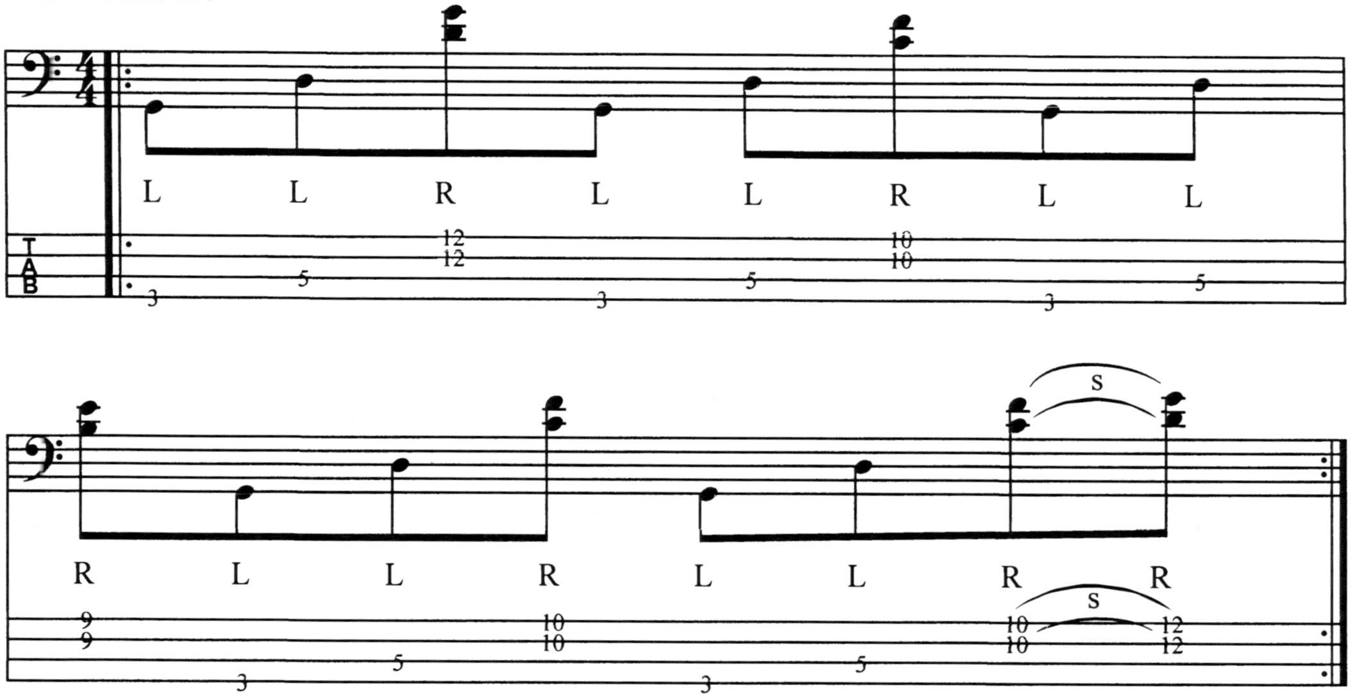

EXAMPLE 46: This example is a twelve bar blues with jazz turnarounds. The right hand plays all the chords above the twelfth fret. The left hand hammers the walking line below the twelfth fret.

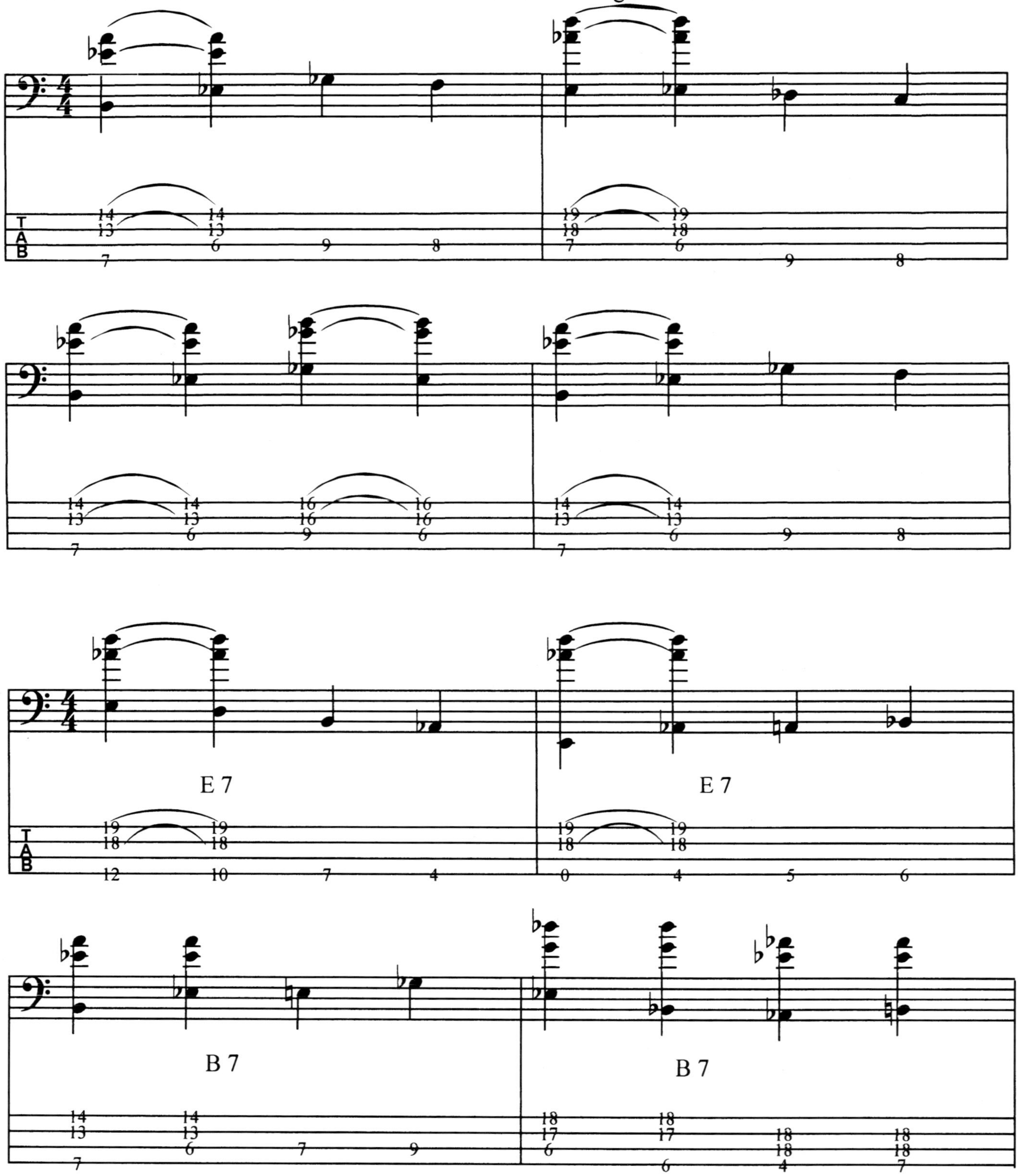

EX. 46 (ctd)

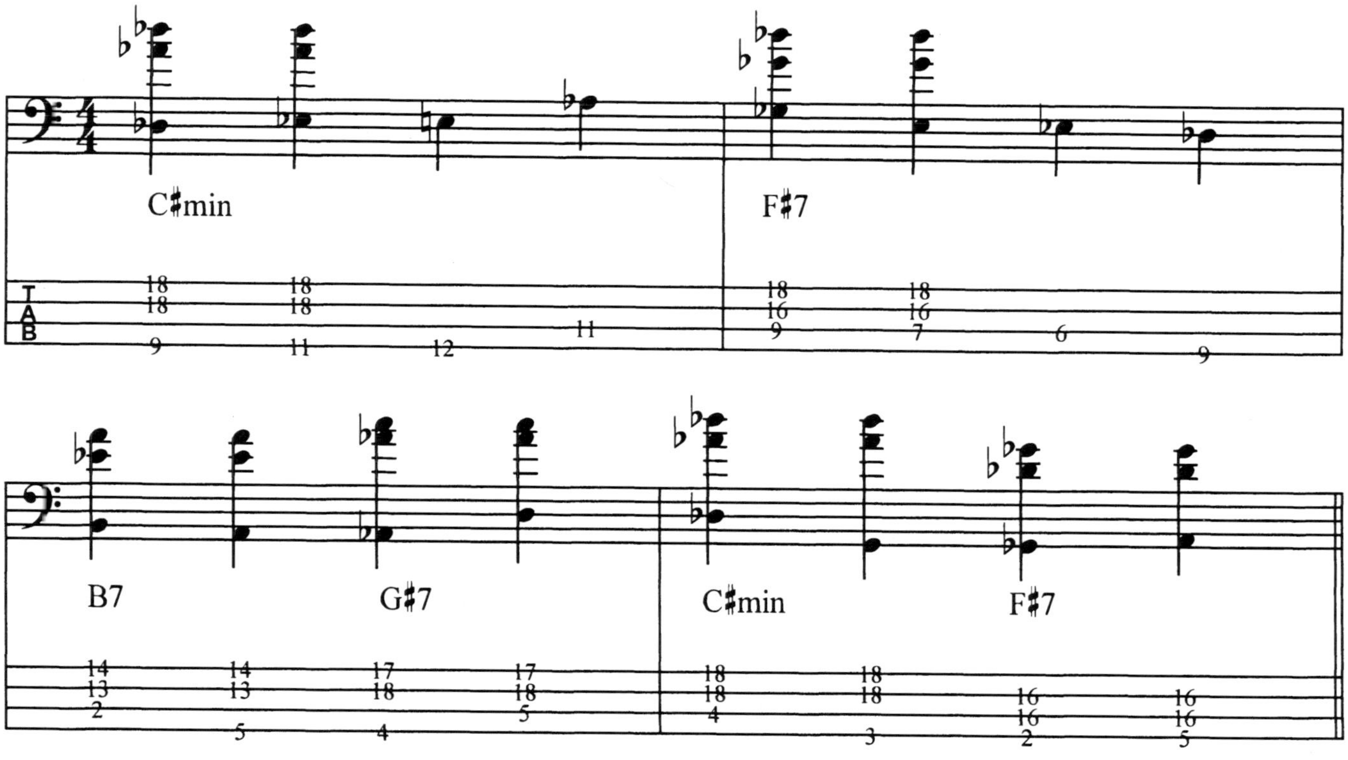

PRACTICE TIP: Examples 46 & 47 are similar to a solo jazz piano part. The left hand plays a walking bass line and the right hand comps chords or melodies. This is a serious workout for any bassist who has not spent a lot of time playing piano. You may want to try working out each part separately before putting them together. Try starting with the walking bass line. Studying piano can help your tapping as well.

EXAMPLE 47:

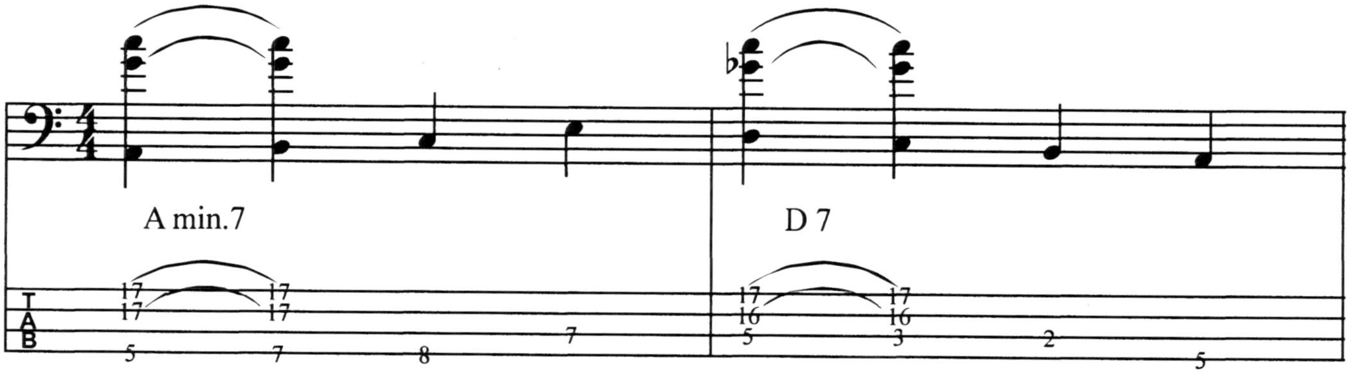

EX. 47 (ctd)

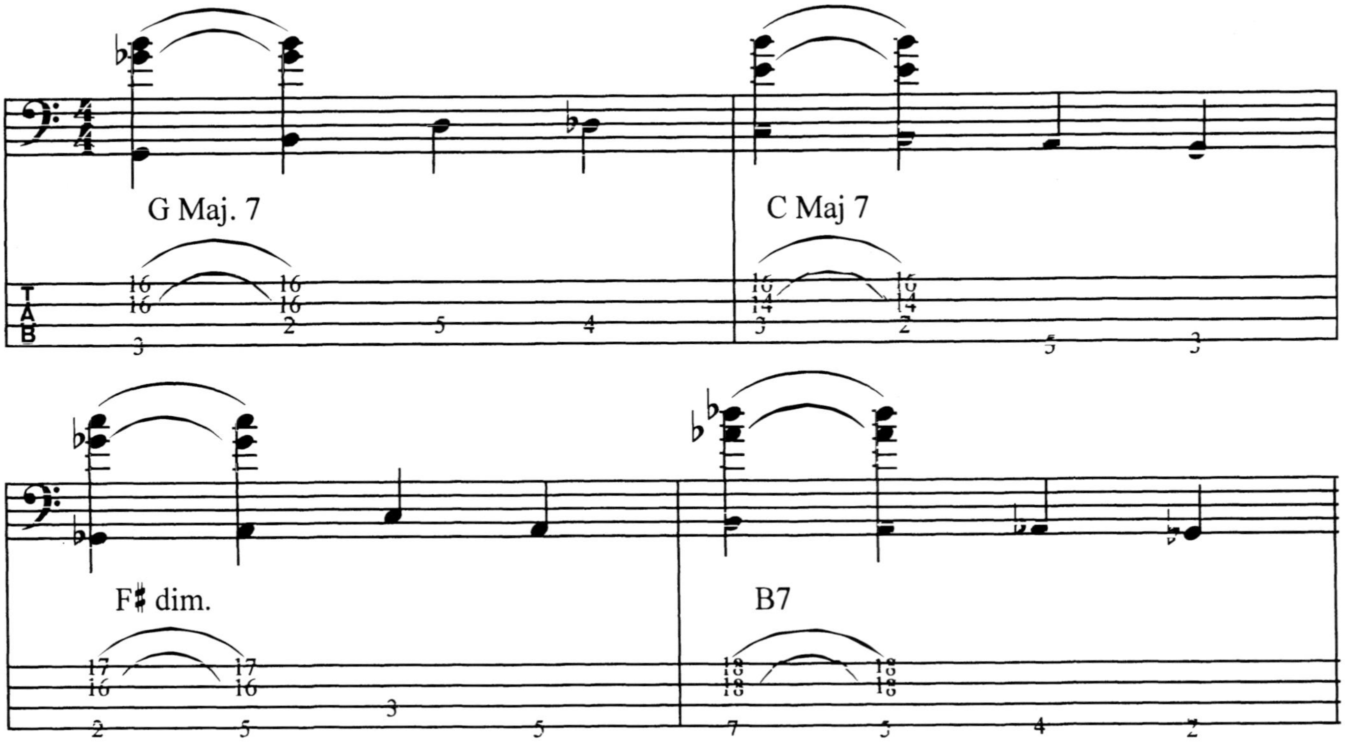

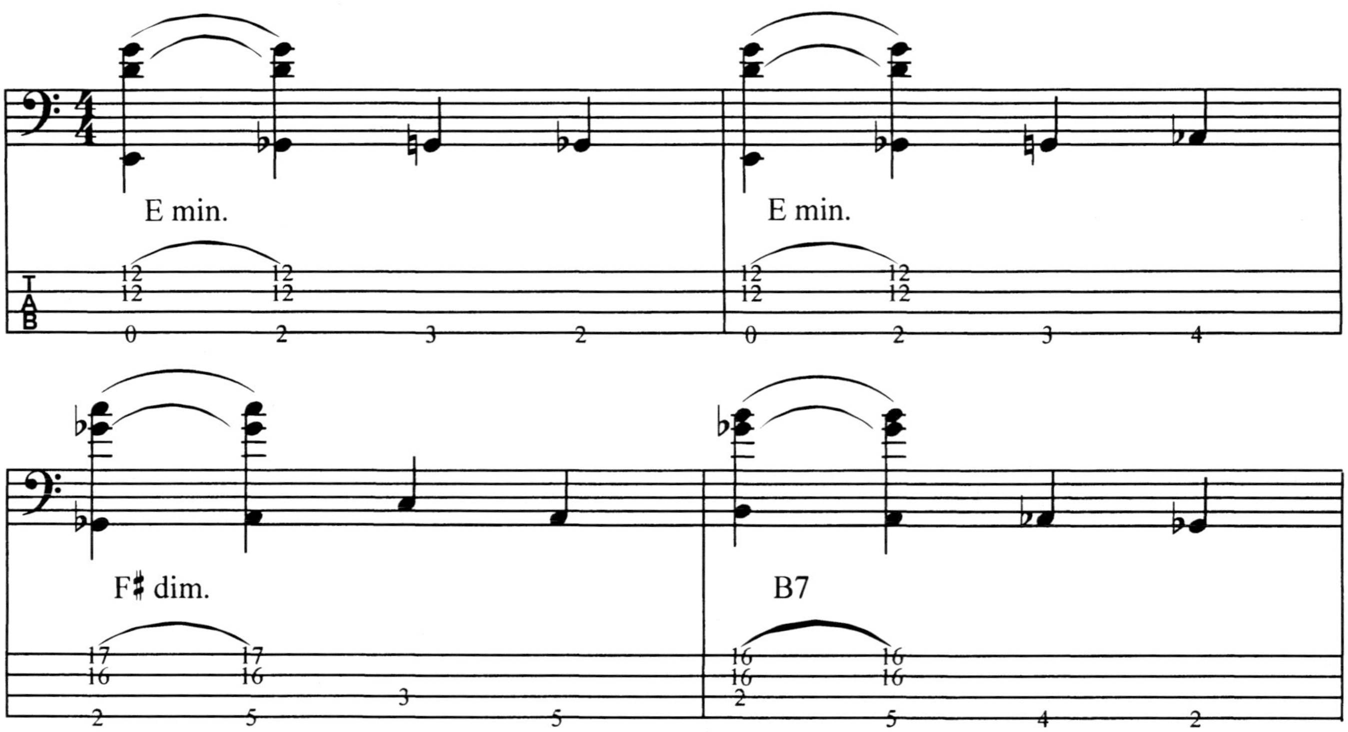

EX. 47 (ctd)

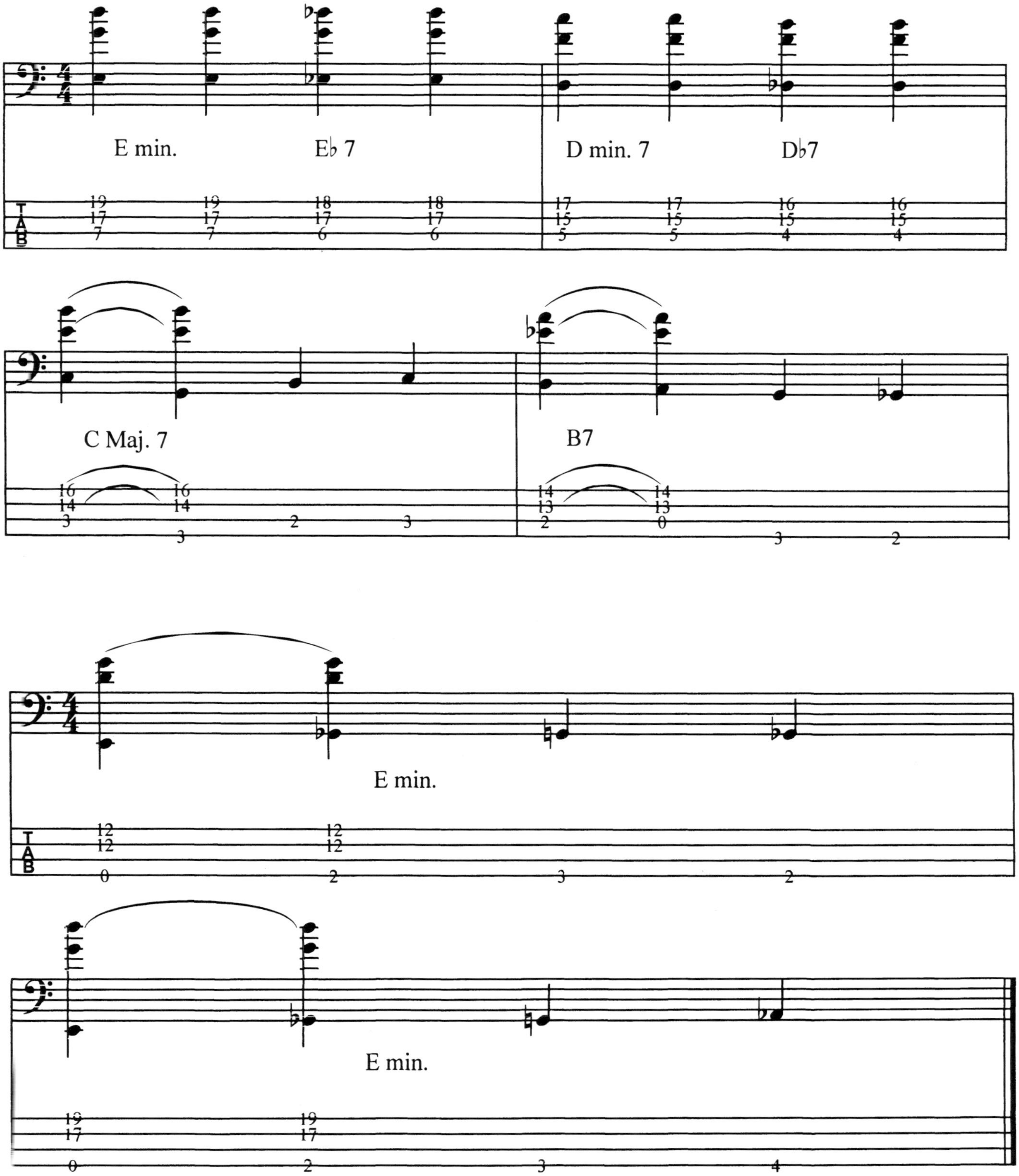

LEFT HAND PINKY

The following example hammers with the left hand pinky. This is nothing unusual with fingerstyle playing. When two-hand tapping with hammers, this takes great hand strength. The right hand taps the notes on the G string.

EXAMPLE 48:

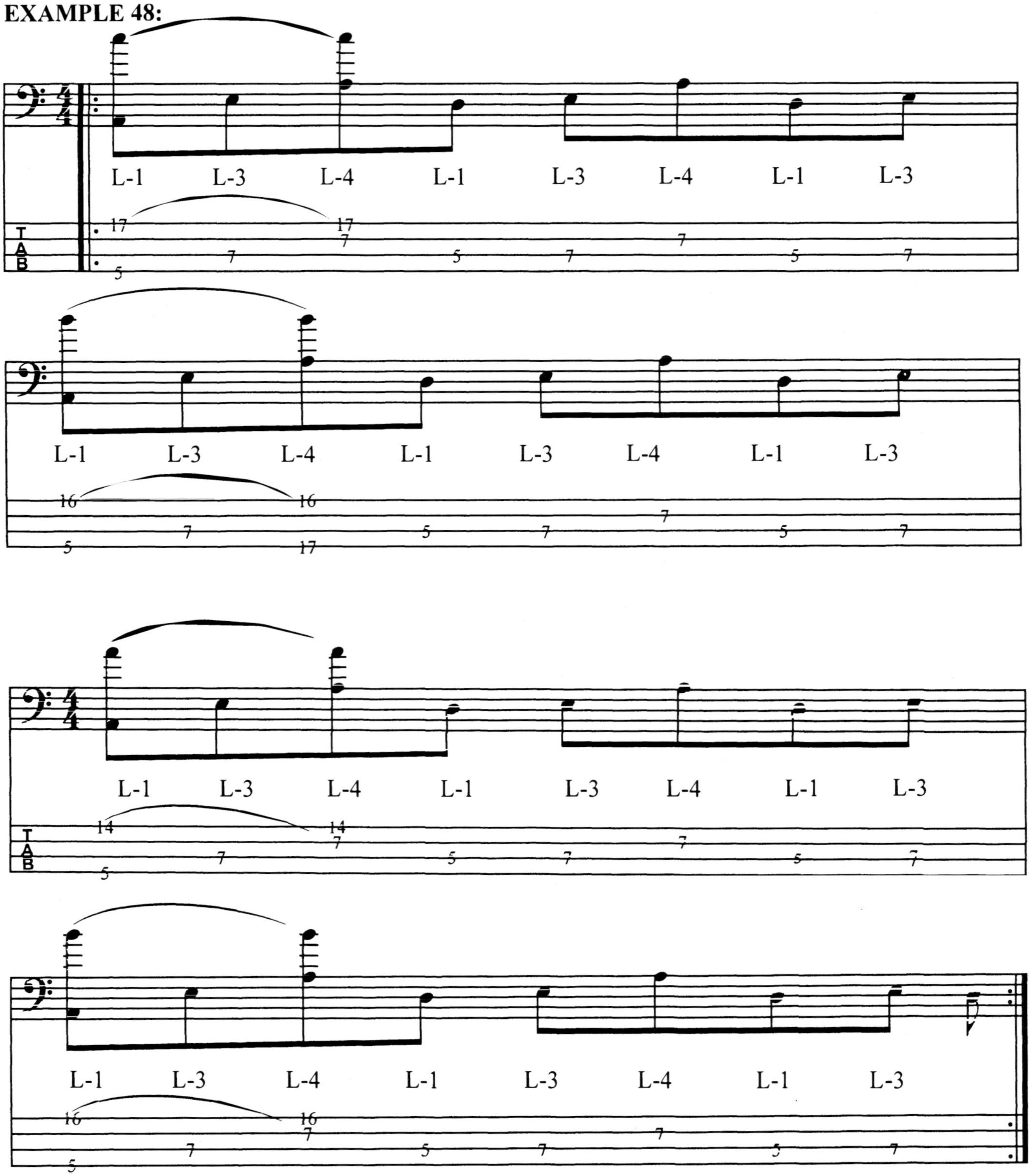

SLIDES

EXAMPLE 49: In this example the slides are played with the right hand.

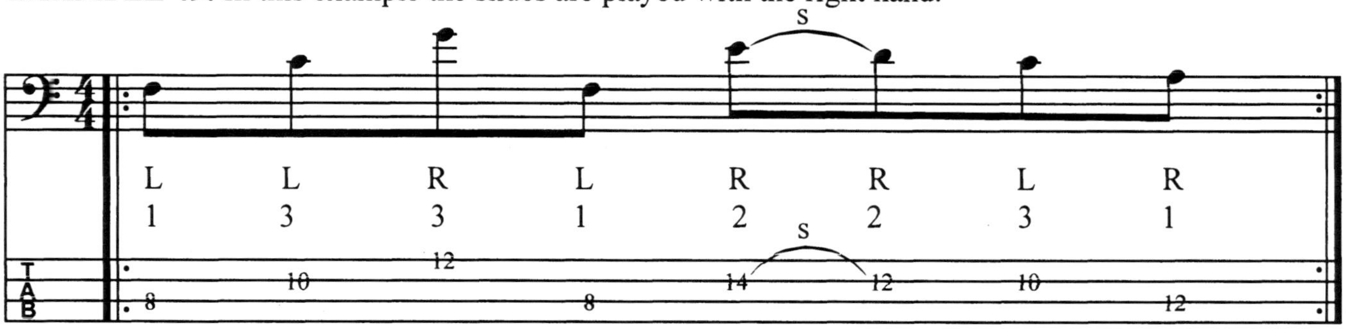

EXAMPLE 50:

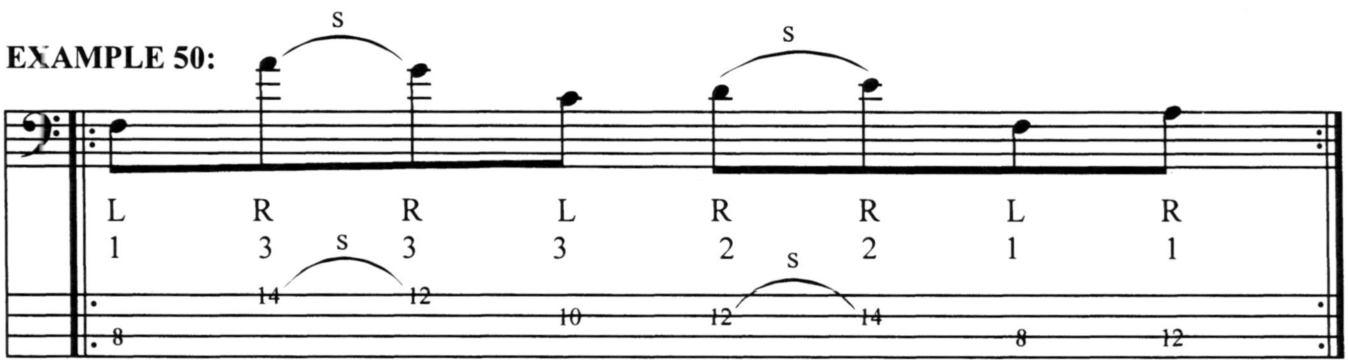

ABOUT THE AUTHOR

CHRIS MATHEOS is a native of Rochester, NY. He studied music at The Berklee College of Music in Boston. He has toured with national acts in about every style of music. He presently endorses Washburn fretted and acoustic basses, Keith Roscoe fretless basses, Bill Conklin electric upright basses, and David Eden Amps and strings. He has written many books for Mel Bay Publications.

other books by Chris Matheos:

Percussive Slap Bass MB95703BCD
Reggae Grooves For Electric Bass............................MB96722BCD
Famous Jazz Bass Chord Progressions MB98582BCD
Famous Rock&Blues Bass Chord Progressions MB98583BCD
Building Amazing Bass Technique MB98434BCD
Bass Warm Ups MB98433BCD
100 Rock n Roll Workouts..MB20703BCD
100 Fretless Bass Workouts MB20702BCD

MEL BAY®